CARE OF THE
RADIOTI

D0634780

Care of the Patient in Radiotherapy

JOYCE N. M. LOCHHEAD

FCR, TDR, Dip Soc
Formerly Superintendent, Radiotherapy Department
Royal Free Hospital, London

Principal, School of Radiotherapy
Royal Free Hospital, London

BLACKWELL SCIENTIFIC PUBLICATIONS
OXFORD LONDON EDINBURGH
BOSTON MELBOURNE

© 1983 by Blackwell Scientific
Publications
Editorial offices:
Osney Mead, Oxford, OX2 0EL
8 John Street, London, WC1N 2ES
9 Forrest Road, Edinburgh,
  EH1 2QH
52 Beacon Street, Boston
  Massachusetts 02108, USA
99 Barry Street, Carlton
  Victoria 3053, Australia

First published 1983

Set by Fourjay Typesetters, Oxford
Printed and bound in Great Britain
by Redwood Burn Limited,
Trowbridge, Wiltshire

DISTRIBUTORS
USA
  Blackwell Mosby Book
    Distributors
  11830 Westline Industrial Drive
  St Louis, Missouri 63141

Canada
  Blackwell Mosby Book
    Distributors
  120 Melford Drive, Scarborough
  Ontario, M1B 2X4

Australia
  Blackwell Scientific Book
    Distributors
  31 Advantage Road, Highett
  Victoria 3190

British Library
Cataloguing in Publication Data

Lochhead, Joyce, N. M.
  Care of the patient in radiotherapy
  1. Radiotherapy
  I. Title
  615.8′42   RM847

ISBN 0-632-01138-6

Contents

Preface

Radiotherapy began in the early part of this century when it was discovered that X-rays brought about changes in tissue growth. To begin with these were not fully understood, and some of the damage and late effects suffered by early pioneers were quite fearful. Even as late as the 1940s, to undergo treatment by 'the deep X-ray' was seen as a last attempt to 'burn the cancer out' – and burn they did, with weeping red skin reactions which made the patient feel ill and miserable and which required daily dressings.

Fortunately this is all in the past. During the Second World War (as is always the case with wars), money spent on research into methods of destruction was repaid when the research brought advances in medicine. The cobalt unit and the precision engineering to arc the treatment head were developed in this way. The use of megavoltage radiation brought a virtual end to the severe skin reactions and diminished other unpleasant side-effects of treatment.

Radiotherapy has now moved into the age of the computer. Already many centres use computer planning systems which enable the time spent on treatment calculations to be reduced considerably. Computerised radiotherapy units are in process of being developed and one is in use at the Royal Free Hospital in London. Computer control enables the irradiated zone to be 'tailored' to the shape of the lesion. The advantage of this is that the dose received by normal tissue may be still further reduced and the patient spared the discomfort of the systemic effects and late radiation damage which in some instances, particularly with carcinoma of the oesophagus, contributes to a poor prognosis.

However, a computer is only the servant of trained personnel. It can only function if the correct information is supplied to it. It cannot care for the patient, answer queries or monitor reactions. Success in radiotherapy depends on good patient care and a great deal of patient care falls upon the radiographer. Radiographers of the future will need to combine considerable technical skills with the human qualities they already possess. This of course is recognised in the plans which are going ahead to increase the training period to 3 years from the present 2.

The field of chemotherapy is also expanding rapidly and radiographers will need to know something about the drugs used in the treatment of cancer and about their effects on the cells and on the patients' systems.

Cancer still remains a cause of fear for a large number of people, but many types of the disease are now curable or controllable. In time it is hoped that public education will help to lessen the fear. Whether we shall ever find a complete cure remains a matter for conjecture. Mr I. G. Williams, who was Director of Radiotherapy at St Bartholomews Hospital, once said 'When we know the secret of cancer, we shall know the secret of life', but I hope that by writing this book I have contributed something worthwhile.

In the course of writing the book, I have referred throughout to the radiographer as 'she'. This is merely for convenience and in no way implies any slight to my male colleagues. Numerically there are more female therapy radiographers than male. As a compensation I refer throughout to doctors as 'he', as is also the case with patients, except where they are obviously female.

It has also been pointed out to me that such organised services and facilities as I have described (ambulance, national follow-up scheme, charities, Acts of Parliament, etc.) are only applicable in the United Kingdom. Similar services probably exist and function abroad. The qualifying examination set by the College of Radiographers, and the Medical Insurance Scheme operated by the Society of Radiographers, is recognised in many parts of the world.

I should like to acknowledge the help and encouragement I have received from many of my ex-colleagues in the preparation of this work, particularly from Dr D. B. L. Skeggs, Director of the Department of Radiotherapy and Oncology, The Royal Free Hospital, London for permission to make use of information and data; Dr F. Senanayake, also of the Radiotherapy Department of The Royal Free Hospital, for his careful reading of the script and his helpful comments; and Miss L. Chadirchi, Superintendent Radiographer of the Radiotherapy Department of The Royal Free Hospital for the same help.

January 1983   Joyce N. M. Lochhead

Chapter 1
The Role of the
Therapy Radiographer

Radiotherapy and other words such as radium and cobalt are associated by many people, quite correctly, with the treatment of cancer. Cancer is a very frightening word. To most people it means a painful and incurable disease and it is unfortunate that this fear sometimes prevents a patient consulting a doctor until forced to do so by pain and disability. By this time the disease is in the advanced stages and the outlook is poor. This applies to other diseases also, but it is a point usually overlooked.

In the radiotherapy department the term 'cancer' is usually avoided. This is partly because it is such an emotive word, but also because it does not mean anything specific. It can be applied to many different tumours.

A more common general term is 'malignant disease'. This also sounds unpleasant and is not used in the hearing of the patient. In the radiotherapy department tumours are referred to by name or, more frequently, as a 'lesion' of the part of the body involved. Malignant disease is potentially a fatal illness, but some malignant tumours, if detected early and given the proper treatment, may be cured – as anyone coming to work in a radiotherapy department will realise. In some cases tumour growth may be arrested and the patient given a number of years of useful and enjoyable life before the disease finally overtakes him. Over the past 20 years or so a great number of discoveries have been made about the behaviour of cells in the body. New diagnostic and treatment techniques have been and are being developed and the scope of radiotherapy and oncology (the study of tumours) is expanding rapidly.

The radiotherapist is a doctor specialising in the treatment of tumours by ionising radiation.

The oncologist is also a specialist in the treatment of tumours. The science of oncology covers every aspect of tumours – their properties, causative factors and treatment.

A radiotherapist may combine oncology and radiotherapy, but in practice oncology is taken to mean the treatment of tumours by drugs (chemotherapy).

The radiographer carries out the radiotherapist's instructions. This is rather different from the role of her diagnostic colleague who offers a service to the hospital by taking films on the receipt of requests from the medical staff.

A therapy dose of radiation may not be given without a signed prescription from the radiotherapist. This is much the same procedure as a nurse must follow when giving a patient a drug. Before a course of radiation treatment is given the dosage and details of field arrangements, etc., are calculated. This is called 'treatment planning'. Treatment planning is a specialised branch of radiotherapy and one in which a radiographer may elect to work as an alternative to carrying out the treatment. Here again, planning procedures are only done on the instructions of the radiotherapist.

Work in the radiotherapy department demands a sound knowledge of the physical principles underlying radiation therapy. It also calls for a high degree of accuracy, attention to detail and personal integrity, for radiation treatment carried out carelessly or wrongly will not only reduce the patient's chances of a cure but can cause disfigurement and even disability. A dose of radiation once given cannot be undone. The effects are permanent.

Radiographers work as a team from two to four in number, depending on the type of unit; this allows an easy working arrangement. It is also a safety factor and one of the reasons that so few mistakes occur because members of the team are able to check each other. Another advantage is that this system helps to maintain staff/patient continuity because it is unlikely that all the members of one team will be absent at the same time.

Successful radiotherapy depends on good patient care. During a course of treatment the patient will experience certain side-effects, some of which will cause him discomfort. The radiographer must be able to anticipate these and recognise them when they occur so that she can advise and instruct the patient, and on occasions the nursing staff, on how to deal with them. This part of the work is extremely important. If a course of treatment is interrupted or not completed in the time planned, the patient's chance of cure may be affected.

The reactions produced by radiation in the tissues of the body are called the biological effect. The biological effect depends as much on the time (or number of days) over which the treatment is given as upon the total dose. The effect on the tissues of a very large dose given in a short period of time will be very different from that produced by giving the same total dose divided into small fractions and spread over a longer period, as anyone can prove for themselves by sunbathing. A dose of radiation is prescribed to be given in a certain number of days. The prescribed number of days includes those on which no treatment is given (weekends and rest days). This is called the overall time.

The radiotherapist sees all patients on treatment at least once each week. For the rest of the time he should be able to rely on the radiographer in charge of the treatment to keep him informed and to draw his attention to any unexpected change in a patient's condition.

TREATMENT POLICY

The treatment of malignant disease is often very complex and prolonged. It requires good liaison between members of the radiotherapy staff and other disciplines in the hospital. Methods of treatment used, either alone or in combination, include surgery, ionising radiation, radio-isotopes and drugs. The method or methods chosen will depend on the type of tumour, its size or extent and its site in the body. At the same time, other factors which may affect the prognosis (expected outcome) must be considered; these include:

(1) Possible disability resulting from the treatment which might spoil the patient's enjoyment of life or his ability to carry on his work. Patients in this situation can be helped by rehabilitation and usually adapt well.

(2) The general condition of the patient. A person who is fairly fit can withstand the rigours of treatment better than one who is weak and ill. In many cases it is possible to bring about an improvement by good nursing care, proper nourishment, control of any infections and blood transfusion prior to starting the course. The general condition also includes the patient's age, but this does not mean that because he is elderly he will not receive a full course of treatment. If other factors are right, he will.

(3) Intercurrent disease. A high proportion of patients attending the radiotherapy department are in the upper age groups and may also have other chronic conditions – cardiac and vascular disorders, respiratory ailments, arthritis, etc. – which may make some modification of the treatment policy necessary.

The treatment policy may be:

(1) Radical – intended to cure. In this case the prognosis must be good. The lesion must be in the early stages or confined to a small

volume of tissue so that it can be treated to a high dose. The side-effects of the treatment, the discomfort of the reactions and the inconvenience of having to attend the hospital daily for 5–6 weeks are considered worthwhile and are accepted as part of the treatment.
(2) Palliative. A cure is not expected but the aim of treatment is to improve the quality of life for the patient by relief and prevention of pain and disability, and by the reduction of other unpleasant symptoms such as ulceration, haemorrhage, difficulty in breathing or swallowing, etc., all of which are exhausting. In this situation side-effects are kept to a minimum because one does not wish to add to the patient's discomfort. The planning is more simple, the course of treatment shorter and the dosage lower than for a radical treatment. The patient may only attend two or three times per week instead of daily. Even when the disease is very advanced, palliative treatment has a good psychological value for both the patient and his family who feel that something is being done and things are not hopeless. In some cases, if the response to treatment is good, the policy may be changed to radical.

RADIOGRAPHER–PATIENT RELATIONS

The patient who comes to the radiotherapy department is naturally apprehensive and the first impression he gets is very important. He will feel much more confident if he comes to a department which is tidy and pleasant in appearance and where the staff give the impression of being efficient and knowledgeable. It is a rather sad fact that many people who are efficient and who work in the public service tend to be bossy. Patients are told 'Sit down there', 'Get undressed', etc., whereas the same instruction accompanied by a smile or a word of explanation and 'please' will be just as effective and put the patient at his ease.

Most patients like to know the radiographer's name and will often ask. It is courteous to introduce oneself. Name badges are also useful in this respect, especially when they show the wearer's rank.

It is equally important for the radiographer to learn the patients' names and to call them by name. It is a courtesy also to try to give a woman the correct title of Mrs or Miss. Some people do not mind – others do.

It is essential that the radiographer should be able to recognise each patient entering the treatment room. This is no mean feat when one remembers that over 50 patients may be treated on one machine each day.

It is not unknown for a deaf or slightly vague patient to answer to the wrong name. Mistakes of this kind are avoidable by asking all patients to present their appointment cards as they enter the room, but the ultimate responsibility rests with the radiographer carrying out the treatment.

During a course of treatment lasting several weeks the patient and the radiographer get to know each other quite well, and it is desirable that there should be continuous patient–radiographer contact. The patient comes to rely on the radiographer in charge of his treatment and feels that she understands it, while the radiographer is better able to observe the patient's progress. Apart from the necessary enquiries regarding the patient's health each day, conversations should be kept to general subjects. Some people have a natural talent for conversation; others find it hard going, but a student ought to try to acquire something of the art, for she must learn to meet and cope with people from all walks of life. Talking to, and general observation of, the patient from day to day is in fact part of the radiographer's job and a great deal of information relevant to the patient's illness can emerge in this way. It is not suggested that the radiographer should pry into the patient's private affairs but her observations should tell her whether he is in difficulties or likely to need help. A long illness or a long course of treatment can create problems quite unforeseen and which can cause a great deal of worry.

Worry can seriously affect a patient's progress and recovery, and people react to it in different ways. Some brood over it by themselves and remain silent and withdrawn. A word with the doctor or with the medical social worker may give the patient a great deal of relief but the necessity for this may have to be brought to their notice. Other people become very talkative when they are worried. The talkative patient is often very nervous or very frightened. The reason for rules of silence in religious houses is that one cannot think and talk at the same time!

Quite often these patients just need a sympathetic listener. Needless to say, the radiographer has not got the time to listen to every patient's troubles. On the other hand, it is bad practice if she has no time to listen at all. Relevant facts often emerge with which the patient 'did not want to bother the doctor'.

From time to time one meets aggressive or difficult patients. Once again this attitude may be due to anxiety. These people are usually highly intelligent and on closer acquaintance prove to be quite different from their first impression. The radiographer must not allow herself to be upset or uncivil but always try to be polite and patient. One has only to imagine oneself in a similar position to realise how worried the patient must be with his whole future and perhaps that of his dependants in the balance.

Our perception of the world around us is governed by several factors – interests, likes and dislikes, state of health, etc., – so that we select some things and ignore others. When a person is threatened by some fear, or is in a state of emotional upset, his perception is distorted and either the fear may become the dominating factor in his life and intrude into everything he does, or he may push it completely out of his mind and pretend that it does not exist. This is done subconsciously, of course. We sometimes meet patients with advanced ulcerated tumours who do not seem to have the least idea of the nature of their condition and who even appear stupid. In fact they may have erected their own mental block and to try to remove this protective barrier could do the patient a great deal of harm.

Other patients, whose perception is heightened by their fear, are sometimes more difficult to deal with. They are constantly seeking clues and scraps of information and will sometimes put the wrong interpretation on things they overhear. A quite harmless remark may be misinterpreted and one must always be careful about what is said in their hearing. These people especially need reassurance and explanation of what is to be done and why.

At all times, private conversation should be discreet and if a patient is present, it is kind to include him so that he does not feel ignored. There should be no element of discord or argument overheard by the patient; neither should there be any criticism of other members of the staff. The patient hopes that he has come to the best place for his treatment, for upon it his life depends and nothing must be done to shake his confidence.

It is not advisable for a student or a junior radiographer to spend a long time alone talking to a patient or make a special friend of one, no matter how sympathetic she may feel. Relationships in the radiotherapy department tend to be more informal than in the diagnostic department, but it is essential to preserve some professional detachment.

Work in the radiotherapy department is both physically and emotionally demanding. It requires a great deal of concentration and to be able to give of her best, the radiographer must be able to maintain a balanced view of life. She must have some outside interests and regular spells of relaxation. The system common to most departments where the staff periodically move from one unit to another is intended to contribute to this by creating a change of interest.

PATIENTS' QUESTIONS

A question that is often asked by students coming into the radiotherapy department for the first time is: 'Does the patient know he has cancer?'. Or alternatively, 'How does one tell him?'. The answers to these questions are:

(1) The patient often has some idea of the nature of his illness.
(2) One does not confirm it in plain words.

A patient who is referred to the radiotherapy department may have had a major operation, such as a mastectomy (removal of the breast) or a fairly small one like an E.U.A. (examination under anaesthetic) and biopsy (removal of a small piece of tissue for examination under the microscope). The need for further treatment is explained to the patient by the consultant, but the word 'cancer' is rarely mentioned. However, no matter how tactfully the necessity for treatment is explained, the patient may realise that he must have a serious condition to warrant a long course of treatment of a type associated with cancer. Many patients ask the doctor directly, and it is instructive to note the way in which the question is usually phrased. 'I haven't got cancer have I?' or 'It's not cancer is it?'. By asking a negative question the patient is hoping that the doctor is going to say 'No'.

An important part of the student radiographer's training is attendance at clinics when patients are seen by the radiotherapist. By doing so she will be able to listen to the patient's questions and the doctor's replies. The radiotherapist knows from his medical experience just how much to tell the patient and how much to withhold. He must also make his answers convincing, or the patient will realise that he has been told nothing and will suspect the worst. The kind of explanation he will give may be something like the following:

'The growth was malignant, but has been *completely* removed. The treatment is recommended as a safety measure. This is called prophylactic (preventive) treatment.'

or:

'The tumour showed pre-malignant or potentially malignant changes. The treatment is recommended to prevent recurrence'.

These statements are generally true and the patient is convinced because he feels the doctor has not tried to hide the truth. In other cases a slightly more vague explanation is given. For example: 'The glands are inflamed and the treatment will reduce the inflammation'; or 'The bones are weakened and inflamed and the treatment will stimulate healing and reduce the pain.'

Every radiotherapist has his own way of putting things. The patient is not told the exact nature or pathology of the tumour. In most cases the pathology would mean nothing to him and it would be both unkind and harmful to frighten him. It is sufficient that he is given hope and the confidence that he is having the best possible treatment. Even when asked directly, a doctor will rarely commit himself to telling a patient how long he has to live. No-one can forecast the length of life: a patient may live by sheer willpower or die much sooner than expected. Even when the prognosis is poor and the radiotherapist knows the patient has at the most only a few months left, it is better that he remain in ignorance lest those months are spoiled by regret.

Inevitably, some patients will also question the radiographer. In general, not many do so, but it requires some experience to be able to handle the situation. It is for this reason that the radiographer should know what the patient has been told or what the radiotherapist is likely to have said so that she can back up his statement in her reply. She must not tell the patient his diagnosis. Only the radiotherapist may take the responsibility for this, as the outcome can be serious. Cases of suicide do occur, although in fact the suicide incidence among cancer patients is lower than that in the rest of the population. To say one is 'not allowed' or 'not qualified' to discuss the patient's condition will often confirm his fears and give him the answer is seeking.

The most common type of question asked by patients is: 'Is this type of treatment always given for cancer?' The answer is of course 'no'. Radiotherapy may be used to treat non-malignant conditions and cancer may be treated by other means.

The patient who asks questions about his diagnosis should be referred to the doctor, but not in a way which implies that the radiographer does not wish to discuss the matter, or that there is any secrecy. For example, the radiographer may say: 'Has the doctor not explained the treatment to you?' or 'Have you not had the opportunity to talk to the doctor? Would you like to?'

In many cases the patient would like the opportunity to talk, and talking to the patient is part of the doctor's job. He will always find time to discuss the patient's illness and treatment with him if the patient wants to.

SOME PROBLEMS OF COMMUNICATION

Deafness

When a patient is deaf and has not got an efficient hearing aid, communication can be very difficult indeed. It is in fact, made worse if the patient is worried and making a special effort to try to hear and understand. Many deaf people find their disability becomes greater in this situation.

A deaf person should not be rushed. He should be taken aside and allowed to relax a little before being questioned or given instruction. The idea that there is plenty of time is important to him.

Many deaf people can lip-read. The speaker should face the patient and speak fairly slowly, while forming the words carefully. A moderately pitched voice is sometimes heard more easily than a shout, which tends to distort the words and in some cases the patient will hear a familiar voice more easily than a strange one. If the information can be given to a relative or a friend, the patient will have the opportunity to have everything made clear later on. It is of course important to make sure that the person to whom the information has been given clearly understands what has been said. Verbal instructions should in any case be accompanied by written ones.

Language

When a patient cannot speak English and cannot explain himself to the doctor or understand what is to be done to him, the process of treating him and gaining his co-operation is very difficult indeed. The patient will also become worried and depressed. If a member of staff speaks even a little of the patient's language, this should be encouraged. It pleases the patient enormously and encourages his co-operation. He may have a relative or friend who speaks English. In this case all communication can be carried on through this person, though it is as well to make sure that he does in fact understand all that is said to him!

Failing this, efforts must be made to find someone in the hospital who can interpret. When details of a patient's medical history are to be taken it is preferable that the interpreter should have some medical or professional training. In large hospitals there are usually some doctors, nurses and technical staff from abroad and in some cases the Personnel Department or the Administration hold lists of linguists. It must be remembered, however, that these people have their own duties to perform and cannot be called upon at short notice and at any time.

There are also many foreign workers in most hospitals who are employed as kitchen staff and porters. Many of them speak good English, but on the whole they lack the education and professional training to act as interpreters for patients from whom intimate personal details are to be obtained. Their services are, however, very useful to find out if the patient has relatives or friends who can act in this capacity and to obtain non-confidential information.

Professional interpreters can be obtained through agencies, but their services have to be paid for and they can be quite expensive. With a bit of imagination, other sources of help can be found in the district around the hospital. Many patients from Mediterranean countries are Roman Catholics and the Roman Catholic chaplain may be able to find someone of suitable standing. Similarly with the Greek Orthodox Church. In London the Embassies of the Arabic-speaking countries have proved helpful. It is also worth approaching advisory centres for different nationals. The local newspaper and the public library are sources of information.

PROFESSIONAL RESPONSIBILITY

The radiographer, in common with other people working in a hospital, has duties and responsibilities towards the patient and to his or her colleagues. A professionally trained person maintains a certain standard of behaviour and will conscientiously carry out the duties he or she has undertaken. This is an *ethical responsibility*. During training the student should always aim at a high standard of knowledge and technical skill. The qualifying examination of the College of Radiographers and acceptance for registration by the Council for the Professions Supplementary to Medicine aim at maintaining this standard.

The radiographer's education does not end with qualification. Research into the treatment of malignant disease continues unceasingly, and as more knowledge is acquired, techniques and methods of treatment change, sometimes with alarming rapidity. A radiographer has a responsibility, therefore, to try to keep up to date with current thought by reading, by attending postgraduate courses and lectures, and by contributing from her own experience.

LEGAL RESPONSIBILITY

Besides ethical responsibility, there are also legal obligations. A patient expects to be taken care of while he is in the hospital and has a right to be looked after. It is in this right that legal responsibility rests. There are three aspects of legal responsibility.

(1) Negligence

Negligence means that there has been a breach of duty owed to someone and, as a result of this breach, damage which was foreseeable has occurred.

The patient has a right to care, and it can be foreseen that serious harm can come to a sick person if he is left unattended or if proper care is not exercised by those carrying out his treatment. A legal action against those responsible may be brought by the person whose right has been breached.

The greatest care must be taken that such incidents do not happen. A radiographer must give all her attention to the job in hand and not allow her attention to be diverted while treating a patient. Students are not permitted to treat patients unsupervised. They are not covered by a professional qualification and are not insured.

Anyone using ionising radiation has a responsibility towards other personnel and to the general public. To use such radiations without due regard to safety is negligent. The rights of the unborn child are protected in law. The risk of foetal damage in the radiotherapy department is not very great (though it does arise occasionally). Due care must be taken to shield the gonad areas of young patients whenever possible. A patient cannot be treated without consent, either his own or, if he is a minor or unable to give it because of his illness, that of his family. Most patients give consent willingly. However, with some forms of treatment, particularly radiotherapy, there are inevitable and permanent side-effects which must be explained to the patient before the treatment is given. These can include baldness following irradiation of a brain lesion, the possible need to sacrifice a vital organ such as an eye, or damage to the reproductive organs in order to treat a tumour adequately and cure him of his disease. In these cases the doctor has a duty to discuss the risks with the patient and, as with the administration of an anaesthetic, the patient's written consent is required.

(2) Accident

An accident is an unforeseen or chance occurrence which may happen in the most carefully regulated department. Should an accident happen, even a minor one, the proper care and treatment must be given and the patient should be seen by a medical officer before being allowed to leave the hospital.

An accident report form must be completed as soon after the incident as possible, giving a full account of what happened. This report is kept by the Administrator of the hospital and is required in case the patient suffers any late effects or subsequent illness which may be, or may be claimed to be, attributable to the accident.

From time to time a mistake may be made in a patient's treatment. Mistakes are in fact quite rare, but if a mistake occurs it must be reported to the Head of the Department, or other appropriate person (radiotherapist or physicist) immediately it is discovered. By so doing, harm can usually be averted by alteration of the treatment plan. To try to conceal a mistake can cause much more harm to the patient, and will be a serious reflection on the integrity of the person involved.

(3) Breach of professional confidence

All information concerning a patient's illness, and all details of his private affairs which may be recorded in the case history, are confidential and may not be disclosed to unauthorised persons. Legal action may be taken against anyone doing so, or using the knowledge for his own advantage.

A patient's written consent must be obtained before details of his illness may be disclosed to any but his next of kin. For example, his employer may wish to know what he is suffering from and how long he is likely to be away from work.

Case histories which are sent from one part of the hospital to another should be put into sealed envelopes.

A doctor will rarely discuss a patient on the telephone, especially with a relative, unless he is sure that the person on the other end of the line is the person he says he is.

When any medical material is used for teaching purposes – X-rays, photographs, etc. – the identity of the patient is concealed or removed.

Legal action brought by patients is commoner now than it once was. The complexity of modern treatment makes the risks greater, especially when drugs are used in conjunction with radiotherapy and patients are treated on units with high dose rates. The Society of Radiographers has an insurance scheme to assist radiographers who may be unfortunate enough to be involved in a legal action, and it is advisable to contribute to it.

Chapter 2
Referral of Patients;
Appointments and Patient Records

REFERRAL OF PATIENTS

A patient who requires treatment for a malignant condition will be referred to the radiotherapist by another consultant (physician, surgeon or occasionally a G.P.) with the request that he will see the patient and give his opinion as to the most suitable treatment. In most cases he will also be asked if he will agree to undertake the treatment. Once the radiotherapist has seen the patient and agreed that he is able to treat him, he will accept him and treat him by whatever means he thinks will be in the patient's best interest. The decision is his, and not that of the referring consultant.

In some cases the radiotherapist will decide that he cannot help the patient. When this happens he will say so and refer the patient back to the original consultant with his reasons and possibly other suggestions.

This procedure is a major difference between the radiotherapy department and the diagnostic X-ray department. The diagnostic X-ray department offers a service to the medical staff of the hospital and to the G.P.s outside the hospital. The patient is not referred, but sent with a request that certain X-ray investigations be carried out.

The radiologist is a doctor specialising in the diagnosis of injury and abnormal conditions from X-ray films. He will give a report on the films and this is sent back to the doctor requesting the investigation. Unlike the radiotherapist, the radiologist only actually sees a small proportion of the patients who come to his department.

WARD ROUNDS

The patient who is referred to the radiotherapist may be in a ward in the hospital, in which case he will be seen initially on the radiotherapist's ward round. Ward rounds take place at a fixed time

14

each week, when the consultant visits all the patients in the wards who are under his care. On the round he is accompanied by several members of his staff and possibly some students. Among these are:

(1)   a registrar – an assistant doctor, junior to the consultant;
(2)   the houseman – a junior doctor who is gaining experience;
(3)   a member of the radiotherapy staff – possibly a radiographer – who can take back information to the department;
(4)   a secretary to take notes;
(5)   the ward sister.

The purposes and advantages of a ward round are:

(1)   it takes place at a fixed time each week, so arrangements can be made to have the results of any tests or X-rays which the patient may have had available for the consultant to see;
(2)   the various members of the staff who are either directly concerned with the patient's treatment, or who can take information back to those who carry it out, are present;
(3)   the consultant can see new patients, review the condition of those already undergoing treatment and receive information regarding their progress. He can give instructions on the continuance or change in the regime to all concerned.

A ward round can also be used for teaching. A student radiographer can learn a great deal in this way.

OUT-PATIENT CLINICS

Patients attend clinics by appointment. As with the ward round, clinics are held at fixed times. This enables the doctor to organise his day and ensures that he will be available to see the patient when he attends. The clerical staff arrange for the case histories and other relevant data to be available.

The disadvantage of an appointment system and clinics at fixed times is that a patient who is seriously ill may not be seen quickly, because clinics are booked up weeks ahead. This problem is overcome by the system operative in many radiotherapy departments where clinic appointments are made by the clerical staff of the department and not by the Out-patients Appointments Department. It is more economical of time to deal directly with the patient and, should a patient have to be seen with the minimum of delay, the radiotherapy staff are better able to judge the degree of urgency.

PATIENT RECORDS

All patients attending a hospital have a case history or file. This document contains the patient's personal details, the history of his illness and a record of the treatment he has received. Case histories are kept by the Medical Records Department. They are filed numerically and the number allocated to the patient must be used on all documents pertaining to him. It is recorded on his appointment card and he should be asked to produce this every time he attends. This number is a means of positive identification. Many people have the same name and live at the same address. Even greater confusion could arise with overseas patients.

The reasons for keeping records are in the main fairly obvious. A doctor cannot remember the details of every patient he has seen. He will need to know what has gone before and to record his own findings and his intentions regarding treatment. This enables patient care to continue without interruption even though changes of staff may occur.

Very often a quick glance through the notes will remind the doctor of some small personal detail which will enable him to greet the patient like an old friend. This flatters the patient and makes him feel that he is an individual in whom the doctor (or the radiographer) has a personal interest.

Some forms of treatment, including radiotherapy, bring about permanent changes in the tissues. These may take many months to become apparent and details of the treatment must be accurately recorded so that the changes can be assessed.

The Radiotherapy Department keeps a separate set of records for patients undergoing treatment and this set of records generally never leaves the department. It includes the relevant medical details from the patient's case history (in case this should be lost or mislaid) and the *radiotherapy treatment sheet*. This has three functions:

(1) it is a prescription for treatment – as such it must be completed with the patient's personal details and signed by the radiotherapist before treatment can be given;

(2) it contains details of the plan of treatment and the data which will enable this to be carried out;

(3) it is a day-to-day record of the treatment. The dose given and the area treated must be entered in ink by the radiographer at the time of treatment, and the entry signed.

PATIENT FOLLOW-UP

Patients who have undergone treatment for a malignant tumour attend follow-up clinics for a considerable period of time. The first attendance is usually within a few weeks of the completion of the course, when the radiotherapist is able to assess the initial response of the tumour to treatment and the reactions in the normal tissues. Subsequent appointments are made at gradually lengthening intervals until the patient is attending annually and will continue to do so for 5, 10 or more years, depending on the type of tumour and the likelihood of recurrence. Success in the treatment of malignant disease is expressed in the number of years the patient has remained free of disease after treatment.

THE NATIONAL FOLLOW-UP SCHEME

The national follow-up scheme is a statistical scheme organised by the Department of Health and the Medical Research Council to register all patients with malignant disease. The register is maintained by follow-up clerks employed in the hospital and records patients' survival and death.

The purpose of the scheme is to correlate the efficacy of the various methods of treatment. Information extracted from the patients' histories is also used to measure the incidence of the disease in various parts of the country and in different sections of the population. From time to time National Surveys of Population Health are published. The Medical Research Council may also ask for the co-operation, from time to time, of departments in the hospital in carrying out a survey. For example, an investigation was done into the effects of the contraceptive pill and its possible relationship to breast cancer.

Medical records are strictly confidential documents. They are only available to those members of the hospital staff who have need of access to them and a high standard of discretion is expected of these persons.

PERSONAL DATA IN MEDICAL RECORDS

Personal details should always be obtained from the patient if possible, and not copied from other documents: this helps to eliminate clerical errors. The patient should also have the opportunity of giving his personal details in privacy. Many people dislike making their date of birth and home address known to anyone who may be listening, including possible burglars. Alternatively he can be asked to write them down. The personal details required are as follows:

Name

The surname and first name. 'First' name is preferable to Christian name because people are not all of the same religion. It is important to check both the spelling and pronunciation.

Address

Again it is very important to check that this is correct. Many wasted ambulance journeys have resulted from incorrect or incomplete addresses. A telephone number is also useful. There may be occasion when the patient has to be contacted at short notice for admission to a ward or because of breakdown of the treatment unit.

Date of birth

This is the most accurate way of determining a patient's age. Other reasons for obtaining it are:

(1)   the doctor needs to know it, and it may have a bearing on the patient's condition and on the treatment he receives;
(2)   it is a means of identification, especially when there are two people of the same name;
(3)   age groups are one of the bases of national surveys which are carried out by the Department of Health from time to time on population health.

Marital status: i.e. married, single, widowed or divorced

This is a guide to the patient's home circumstances and financial state. It may also have a link with the state of health. Environment affects our physical well-being, and a patient with a wife or a husband who will give help and support in illness will respond more quickly than a lonely person living by himself.

Next of kin

It is essential to know someone, preferably related to the patient, but not necessarily, whom the hospital can contact. There are several reasons for this:

(1)   the patient may not be able to give information about himself;
(2)   in cases of serious illness, the relative must be told – even when the expected outcome is not serious, it is usual for the doctor to explain the nature of the illness to the relatives so that they may give the patient support and sympathy and help in his recovery.

Next of kin relationships are as follows: husband/wife; parent/child; siblings (brothers and sisters); as the patient wishes.

Occupation

The patient's occupation is very important because certain diseases have a direct connection with certain types of work. Pneumoconiosis in coal miners is a well-known example. Where malignant disease is concerned there are some substances which are carcinogenic – cancer-inducing – and workers with these may be at risk.

National Surveys on Population Health look at the degree of morbidity, i.e. the amount of illness and its type in the population in relation to occupation; if a high incidence is found in a particular group, efforts are made to find the reason and to take preventive measures. A patient's place of residence is significant in this respect also.

In the case of women who do not go to work, the husband's occupation should be recorded. If the patient has retired his occupation before retirement should be asked.

A person's occupation also determines his social stratum and this again can have a bearing on his health.

The name and address of his G.P.

The general practitioner has the care of the patient outside the hospital and it is probable that it was he who sent the patient to the hospital. A letter is always sent to him to tell him of the diagnosis and the treatment carried out. In this way the G.P. can co-operate with the hospital. In many cases treatment is continued at home under his supervision and the patient's progress reported to the hospital.

If a patient is very ill, and the prognosis is poor, he will be able to give the family help and advice regarding the nursing and terminal care.

Religion

The patient's religion is recorded in his case history, especially if he is to be admitted to the ward. The hospital has resident chaplains, and many people who are ill like to have the comfort afforded by religion. Some religions have strict rules regarding diet and drugs. Efforts are made to respect these.

Many convalescent homes and nursing homes are run by religious organisations. Patients who require this kind of care usually prefer to go to one which is congenial.

The patient's religion is also required in case of death.

DEPARTMENTAL STATISTICS

The costing, staffing and equipping of a radiotherapy department is measured in terms of work done. This is very difficult and the system is misleading. The amount of work done cannot really be measured in patients because one patient may take 5 minutes to treat whereas another will occupy most of the day.

On the whole, the work of the department is assessed on the number of new patients seen in a year, the number treated and the total number seen by the medical staff. It is a somewhat haphazard system, but means have to be found to judge the amount of equipment needed, the number of staff to run it and consequently the amount of money required by the hospital from the Department of Health to pay for it. No department ever gets all the money it needs and it is encumbent on the staff to be economical of the resources.

PATIENTS' SERVICES

Illness and the necessity of attending hospital, sometimes at a considerable distance, for a prolonged course of treatment, brings unexpected difficulties. There is, however, quite a lot of help available to a patient who needs it, though he may have to be told that it exists.

A medical social worker is attached to the radiotherapy department and she will see every patient who attends, if necessary. Not every patient needs help. Some are quite self-sufficient, while others are reluctant to admit that they are in need. The doctor, the radiographers and the nurses are usually quite good judges of a patient's circumstances.

On the other hand, some patients expect to be given everything and it requires firmness and discernment to refuse unreasonable requests.

A serious illness causes the patient a great deal of worry and this may slow his recovery. The chance to discuss it all with someone who is trained to listen, and who can offer constructive advice, may halve the problem.

A patient may also be in financial need. Earnings can be lost through reduced working capacity, especially if he is self-employed or unskilled, and there will be increased expenses of fares to the hospital and prescriptions.

Apart from financial help through official channels, there are certain charities which will help patients with malignant disease. The National Society for Cancer Relief (N.S.C.R.) is such a one. This Society will make cash grants to patients in need. This is arranged by the medical social worker and the doctor in charge of the treatment, and the patient is not told of the source of the money. The N.S.C.R. also helps to finance research. It is supported by voluntary contributions.

Home help services can also be arranged for people who live alone to enable them to maintain their independence. A home help will assist with day-to-day chores of cooking, shopping and housework. The service is not free but the charges are quite small if the patient has a limited income.

The Meals on Wheels Service is run by the Women's Royal Voluntary Services (W.R.V.S.). Under this scheme the housebound can receive a hot meal two or three times each week, brought to their homes. It is a service of great value, especially to the elderly. Again it is not free but the cost is small.

Other services arranged by the medical social worker include convalescent and nursing home care. After an illness, a convalescent holiday helps to restore the patient to normality. For the patient who is very ill, and whose relatives cannot care for him at home, there are nursing homes.

Many of these nursing homes are run by religious orders and their organisers strongly object to the term 'terminal home' by which they are often known. On average, they are cheerful, pleasant places where the patients receive the gentle nursing care which often prolongs the spell of life left to them.

DISTRICT NURSING SERVICE

The district nurse is part of the community services and can be asked to call on a patient at home for dressings, injections and other nursing care. This is arranged by the nursing staff of the department.

DRUG SEASON TICKETS

Prescription charges for drugs cost the patient quite a lot. These only go a little way, however, towards the actual cost of the drugs dispensed. The pharmacy is one of the most costly departments of the hospital. Some patients are exempt from charges (old age pensioners and some whose life depends on a drug). Other patients can save some of the cost by buying a 'season ticket' to cover the cost of prescriptions for 3 or 6 months. Patients who are being treated for malignant disease may come into this category, and details of the scheme are available from the hospital pharmacy.

PATIENTS' TRANSPORT

The ambulance service and the hospital car service are intended for patients who, because of their physical condition, cannot use the public transport services.

By far the largest number of ambulances coming to the hospital are carrying patients attending for regular weekly or daily treatment. These belong to a special branch of the ambulance service and do not deal with accidents and emergencies. Patients' transport is booked through the transport officer or ambulance liaison officer, as he is sometimes called, working in the hospital. He arranges the transport with the central ambulance control for the district in which the patient lives. Ambulance transport is very expensive and the service must not be used to save the patient paying his fare. If his difficulty is one of finance the medical social worker will help him.

The ambulance service is not controlled by the hospital. It is controlled by the county council and paid for out of the county rates. On average, 48 hours is needed to order an ambulance, except for an emergency. Emergencies are handled by a different branch of the service. The reason for the long delay in booking an ambulance is that there are not enough ambulances and crews to cope with every journey individually, and the control has to plan the work so that patients are picked up on a round trip, as on a bus service. This means, of course, that some patients have quite a long ride. Another disadvantage of the ambulance service is that it can rarely be relied on to bring the patient at a particular time and this, together with the fact that several patients will all arrive together, causes chaos in an appointment system.

In the treatment section of the department this erratic arrival of patients has to be allowed for. The radiographer in charge of a treatment unit makes her own appointments and, knowing the average arrival times of the ambulances, sets aside part of the day for these patients. When transport is booked information on the patient's condition must be supplied – sitting, stretcher, etc., – so that the correct type of vehicle can be sent. It is also helpful if the approximate departure time can be stated, as this may save the patient a long wait for the return journey.

Chapter 3
Care of the Patient in the
Radiotherapy Department;
Prevention of Accidents and First Aid

The safety of the patient while he is in the Radiotherapy Department is of major importance. There are also certain risks to which the rest of the personnel are exposed and these must be recognised if they are to be avoided.

The Health and Safety at Work Act 1974 came into force in April 1975. As a result of this Act, workers come under protective legislation and employing authorities are obliged to provide hygienic and safe working conditions and do all in their power to ensure safe working systems and sufficient information, instruction and training.

The Act also actively involves the work-people themselves. Provision is made for the setting up of a Safety Committee with an elected representative in the department. Staff are expected to be aware of potential hazards and to comply with safe codes of practice. Defects and omissions must be reported to the Safety Officer so that they can be remedied. They are also expected to be familiar with emergency procedures, for example fire drill and first aid, and to develop a personal concern for the safety of themselves and others.

Patients are in general a bad accident risk. They are often bewildered by unfamiliar hospital surroundings. They feel awkward when asked to undress and in their embarrassment they do silly things like putting their feet on the pillow when asked to get on to the couch. Instructions given to them are only half-heard or forgotten, so it is very important to give the patient one's whole attention and to explain carefully what is to happen and what he is expected to do. He must never be made to feel he is being rushed because there is a queue of people waiting, and the radiographer must not show signs of impatience, even though she may feel it!

When a patient is ill, or in pain, he is not able to cope with everything going on around him as well as he might in normal health, and having to answer questions and move about requires a lot of effort.

Analgesics (pain-killing drugs) and sedatives slow the reactions and reduce the ability of patients to do things for themselves, although

24

they are often necessary to enable them to co-operate during the treatment.

The patient may need help to dress and undress. This help should be offered tactfully because he may resent his helplessness, though most patients accept it gratefully. When assisting someone out of his clothes, it is important to remember that the sound limb should always be removed from the garment first. The garment may then be slipped off the painful one. When dressing, the procedure is reversed and the painful limb inserted first. This reduces movement in a painful limb and consequently reduces the risk of injury – an important point when there is a danger of fracture, due to disease in the bone.

Many radiotherapy patients are elderly and have therefore not got the mobility of younger people. In old age the bones lose some of their calcium and may become brittle. When an old person has a fall it very often results in a fracture. Loss of calcium from the bones is called osteoporosis. Osteoporosis may occur as a result of other conditions, one of the most common being a long debilitating illness. Malignant disease, especially in its advanced stages, is such a condition.

Patients who are confined to bed for any length of time lose their muscle 'tone' and feel weak and wobbly when they try to stand. For this reason, patients are mobilised – got up out of bed – as soon as possible after an operation. When the patient cannot be got up, the physiotherapist will visit him in the ward and give him exercises to improve the muscle tone. These exercises may be active, i.e. the patient does them himself, or they may be passive, i.e. the physiotherapist moves the patient's limbs for him if he is unable to do so himself.

Mobilisation and physiotherapy play an important role in the prevention of chest infections in bed-ridden patients.

A second reason for getting a patient mobilised is the psychological effect. Most people feel so much better when up and dressed in their own clothes than when sitting about in a dressing gown. Most hospitals nowadays allow the patient to keep his own clothes in the ward so that he may get dressed as soon as is practicable. This psychological effect, and the feeling of returning to normal, is an important factor in helping the patient overcome the reactions to radiation therapy.

Getting the patient mobile must be done with care. One of the characteristics of a malignant tumour is that it can produce secondary deposits in other parts of the body (see Figure 1). These are

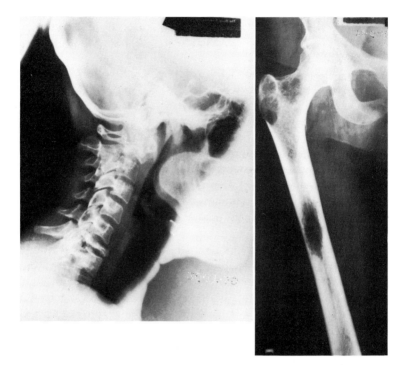

Figure 1. Bone metastases. (By permission of the Radiotherapy Department, Royal Free Hospital, London).

called metastases (singular: metastasis). A metastasis in bone will cause bone destruction and fractures. A fracture resulting from a disease process is called a pathological fracture. Simple weight-bearing on a diseased bone may be enough to cause the bone to break.

Before asking a patient to stand it is important to make sure that he is permitted to do so. Patients should always be given proper support and the floors of the rooms must be kept free of obstacles so that they do not trip. If the patient is wearing a supporting splint or collar, this must not be removed until he is positioned on the couch in such a way that the part is properly supported.

WHEELCHAIR PATIENTS

Patients who are weak or unable to walk unaided are brought to the department in a wheelchair. When the chair is being moved the patient's arms must be inside the arm rests so that they do not get knocked, and his feet must be resting on the foot-rest. If there is a blanket round his knees this must be arranged so that it cannot get caught in the wheels.

When the patient is assisted into or out of the chair the wheels must be locked and the foot-rest folded up or pushed out of the way so that he cannot stand on it and cause the chair to tip forwards. If the wheels cannot be locked, the person assisting the patient should place her foot against the wheel so that the chair does not roll back as the patient sits down.

An ill or elderly patient must never be left unattended while sitting in a wheelchair. Such people frequently doze off. This is the body's way of conserving strength and there is a risk that they may fall out of the chair and sustain an injury.

Before attempting to get a patient on to the couch, the brake on the couch must be applied so that it does not move. Most radiotherapy treatment couches can be lowered to a convenient height for the patient to be able to sit on the edge. If this is not the case, steps of a suitable type must be provided. The type which are easiest to use are on castors which lock when weight is applied.

When the patient is able to stand, he should be told to move to the edge of the couch and swing his feet up into a sitting position, while the radiographer puts a supporting hand behind him to prevent him from overbalancing. He must never be allowed to get onto the couch on all fours. He is much more likely to fall in this position, and will be difficult to catch if he does so. There is also the likelihood that dirt from the floor will soil the sheet as he draws his feet under him and this will increase the risk of infection should there be a wound or skin reaction in the perineal area. Once on the couch, the patient is assisted to lie down by placing a supporting hand behind his shoulders. When the patient gets off the couch again, it is easier and safer if he is assisted directly on to the floor rather than on to steps unless the couch is excessively high.

STRETCHER PATIENTS

A patient who is in pain, or who has bony metastases which are likely to fracture, will probably be safer and more comfortable if brought for treatment on a stretcher. In most cases this will reduce the number of moves the patient has to make, i.e. from bed to chair to couch and back, and it may be possible to give him the treatment without moving him from the stretcher. Although a radiographer should know the correct way to lift a patient, she will not be required to do this very often. Moving patients by lifting them is kept to a minimum because of the risk of pathological fracture or causing the patient pain.

A patient is moved from the stretcher to the couch by means of a canvas and poles. The canvas is a strong canvas or plastic stretcher cover with slots along each side to take lifting poles. The poles are usually made of aluminium alloy and are therefore light to handle in spite of being 7 feet (2.1 metres) long. Occasionally they are made of wood. The poles are pushed through the slots and protrude at either end to form lifting handles.

Spreaders are sometimes used when the canvas has to be kept taut. These are transverse bars which slip over the ends of the poles and keep them apart.

The procedure for removing the patient from the stretcher to the couch is as follows: The couch is adjusted to the height of the stretcher trolley and the stretcher is placed alongside it. The patient is lifted over. One person can usually manage the feet but two people should take the head end. Once the patient is on the couch, the poles are removed.

A more recent development is the Surgilift Trolley which has the advantages of a canvas and poles without the necessity of having to lift the patient and can be operated by one person with safety. The trolley has a radiolucent, removable plastic top which can be positioned over the couch and a facility for height adjustment, enabling the patient to be lowered gently to the couch top.

It is often desirable to remove the canvas or plastic trolley top from under the patient. This may be done without discomfort if the correct procedure is followed. The patient is rolled a little to one side, while someone stands in front of him to prevent him rolling too far. The canvas is folded lengthwise under him. The patient is then rolled to the opposite side and the canvas pulled out. When the canvas is to be replaced the procedure is reversed.

When it is necessary to turn the patient onto his side, the following procedure is used: Two people are required to turn him, one standing on either side of the couch. Bend the patient's knees so that the soles of the feet rest on the couch. Place his hands on his chest. One person places one hand under the shoulders and the other under the buttocks, and gently pulls the patient towards her. The other person places one hand under the head and with the other supports the knees.

Once in position, a pillow placed in front of the body gives support and 'something to hold'. To maintain the position, the knees are bent and a sandbag is placed on the couch between the lower legs, the upper leg being in front of the lower.

HELPLESS PATIENTS

Patients who are unconscious, confused or hemi-plegic must have cot sides on the bed or stretcher to prevent them falling off. Treatment couches are narrower than stretcher tops and do not usually have facilities to fit cot sides. An alternative safety device in the treatment room can be provided by using webbing straps with a quick-release fastening which can be passed round the patient's body and the couch top to give additional support. 'Velcro' stitched to the ends of non-stretch webbing is suitable.

Support of this kind is particularly important for hemi-plegic patients because the weight of a paralysed limb is sufficient to pull the patient off the couch if it should slip over the side and remain unsupported.

Many patients do not like to be brought to the department on a stretcher, particularly if they have been sitting up and getting mobilised. They see it as a retrograde step. The nursing staff share this view and often feel that it is psychologically bad for the patient. There are, however, occasions when the risks and effort of moving a heavy and semi-paralysed patient from a wheelchair to the couch make a stretcher the only practical solution. If the situation is explained to all concerned – the patient and the nursing staff – consent will usually be obtained.

A radiographer should never attempt to handle a helpless patient unaided. Not only is there a risk to the patient, but she may well injure herself also. Strained backs are an occupational hazard among hospital staff and are usually avoidable.

SLIPPED DISC

Prolapsed or slipped disc injury is usually caused by faulty lifting technique when handling heavy weights. The intervertebral discs have a pulpy centre and a fibrous outer cover. When subjected to undue strain the outer cover is damaged and the centre ruptures, producing a bulge over which the nerves are stretched. This causes pain, tingling and weakness in the limb which the nerves supply. The symptoms are increased whenever the nerve is stretched – by bending the back or the limb. The treatment is rest, support and, in severe cases, surgery.

Prevention includes learning the correct lifting techniques and having sufficient help when handling patients.

POSITIONING THE PATIENT ON THE TREATMENT COUCH

Correct positioning of the patient on the treatment couch is of vital importance to the accuracy of the treatment. The patient's position is 'beam directional'. Beam direction is a term applied to any means or device which ensures that the radiation is accurately directed at the lesion. The position is determined at the time the treatment is planned and the lesion localised in relation to other tissues. Should the position of the body subsequently be altered, this relationship will also be altered. The fields will no longer 'fit' and the dose distribution will be wrong. This will have very serious consequences for the patient. If part of the tumour is underdosed it will recur, and radiation changes in the surrounding tissues may preclude further treatment being given.

If too high a dose has been received by a vital organ close to the tumour, the quality of the patient's life may be impaired, even though he is cured of his disease.

Prior to setting up a treatment, it is the radiographer's responsibility to ensure that the patient's position is correct. The patient must be sufficiently uncovered for the treatment area to be clearly seen and it is a good practice to view the patient from the end of the couch to make sure that the body is correctly aligned with the centre of the couch and is not tilted or rotated.

Once the patient is in the correct position, he must maintain it without moving for the duration of the treatment. Immobility is achieved by:

(1) Consent. Consent is necessary before any treatment can be given. A patient cannot be treated against his will (or against that of his family if he cannot give it himself). In cases where treatment will cause inevitable side-effects, written consent is required (see Legal Responsibility).

(2) Comfort and security. Most people can maintain a given position if they are at ease and relaxed. The knowledge that he is under observation for the whole of the time he is being treated gives the patient a sense of safety. Observation via a direct-viewing window enables the patient to see the radiographer. When closed-circuit television is used, the patient should be told.

(3) Various positioning and beam directional aids. Certain items of equipment may be made specifically for the patient as part of the planning procedure, the most usual being beam directional shells. These fit closely over the part to be treated and carry beam directional marks.

The use of such aids does not imply that the patient is subjected to restraint. Restraint induces panic, and self-injury can be caused as a result of struggling. All positioning devices are secured by quick-release clips and the patient can free himself with minimal effort if he wishes to do so. Most patients tolerate such devices well. However some find them uncomfortable and claustrophobic.

CLAUSTROPHOBIA

Claustrophobia is the fear of confined spaces. It is quite common – many people are oppressed by lifts and underground trains and some cannot tolerate them at all. Sometimes patients find the treatment room oppressive, especially megavoltage rooms where there are no outside windows. Restraint around the head and neck makes the condition worse.

Most people who suffer from claustrophobia can overcome their fear, but a small percentage cannot. The fear is very real and the patient must be handled with sympathy and understanding. During treatment, close supervision is essential. An electric fan in the room creating a slight draught gives the impression of airiness and if necessary the doctor may prescribe mild sedation.

The claustrophobic impression given by a megavoltge room can be reduced by the use of pleasant light colours in the decoration and good ventilation. Some account of this is taken in the design of modern treatment units to make them appear less massive.

SAFETY IN THE TREATMENT ROOMS

The patient is understandably apprehensive at the first sight of the treatment room and the knowledge that he is to be left alone in it.

When the patient is on the couch, the radiographer in charge of the controls of the motor-driven equipment must pay full attention to the job in hand, both for the safety of the patient and the care of the equipment. Particular care is necessary in arcing and rotational techniques, in which the treatment head is moving throughout the time of the treatment. It is absolutely essential to 'sweep out' the path to be covered by the head before treatment is carried out to ensure there is no risk of collision. A cobalt 60 head weighs over a ton.

Motor-driven equipment must never be left in a condition in which it can be operated by unauthorised people. The operational key must be removed to the key cupboard when the unit is not in use.

All treatment units are serviced regularly and any minor fault must be recorded in the log book. The log book of a treatment unit is an official document. It is initiated when the machine is new and remains with it until it goes for scrap.

All accessory equipment used in the treatment room must be kept clean and stored in the correct manner to prevent damage. Items attached to the treatment head, such as beam directional cones, must be securely fastened before they are positioned over the patient and it is inadvisable to hand any object, such as a sandbag, over the patient's body in case it is accidentally dropped.

LEAD SHIELDING IN THE TREATMENT ROOM

Lead (Pb) of the appropriate thickness for the beam energy is used to shield organs in the vicinity of the lesion when required. In the lower energy ranges the thickness of the lead is from 0.5 to 2.0 mm. For shielding against gamma (γ) radiation, blocks of lead or lead alloy of 5–6 cm are required.

Thin lead shielding (up to 2 mm) may be placed in contact with the skin. Lead masks may be made to facilitate the treatment of small irregularly shaped skin tumours, especially of the face where beam directional accuracy is essential and skin marks are difficult to maintain. Small lead shields are also inserted into the mouth or nostril to protect the mucosa and under the eyelid to protect the parts of the eye (see Care of the eye). Lead is a poisonous metal, and when it is handled, small deposits rub off on the skin. Lead used in the treatment room is painted or varnished. Cellulose paint in spray cans is suitable and convenient.

Lead shields introduced into a body cavity must be covered with a rubber sheath. Finger cots are usually suitable, but larger sheaths may be obtained from the instrument curator of the hospital if required.

When lead shields are used in the nose or mouth they are drilled and threaded with tape which is in turn taped to the skin or attached to the pillow when the shield is in position. This is to prevent the shield being inhaled or swallowed. The patient is usually treated lying down, and it is easy for small object to slip into the throat.

Lead blocks used for shielding against gamma radiation are supported on a carrier attached to the treatment unit and positioned by the shadow they cause in the diaphragm light.

Lead is a soft metal and thin sheets suffer metal fatigue by being bent and straightened constantly, with eventual cracks. Pieces of lead should be screened periodically at the kilovoltage for which they are intended to be used, and faulty lead discarded. This applies also to protective lead rubber clothing supplied for the use of staff and others in certain situations. Large blocks of lead must be handled with care to avoid damage to the edges and corners which will impair their shielding efficiency.

After handling lead, the hands should be washed with soap in cold water. Lead is slightly soluble in hot water and hot water opens the pores of the skin.

ACCIDENTS AND FIRST AID

The number of accidents which can happen in a radiotherapy department are fairly limited. Furthermore, being part of a hospital with help fairly close at hand, first aid measures will only have to be given for a comparatively short time. There are two important points to be remembered.

(1)   No matter how small the accident to a patient, it must never be ignored. The proper care and attention must be given and a report made on the incident.

(2)   In any serious incident or major accident, sending for help is an essential first step. No matter how good the first aid being given, in certain situations specialised medical care is vital to the patient's life.

Sending for help does not mean abandoning the patient. It is unlikely that a radiographer will be alone in the department and, in the absence of someone else in the room, calling out will bring an assistant. Treatment rooms are fitted with pushbutton-operated alarms and the radiographer must be familiar with their location. These are also to be found in patients' toilets, cubicles and other clinical rooms. A hospital also has an emergency internal telephone number. This is printed on all telephones and should be known by all personnel.

In all cases it is essential to remain calm and not communicate alarm to the patient.

The following emergencies are those most likely to occur:

Fracture

In the radiotherapy department the most likely cause of a fracture will be a bony metastasis, despite care and precautions taken. A pathological fracture of a long bone is just as much a traumatic experience for the patient as a fracture from any other cause.

Signs of fracture

Pain and swelling at the site; deformity or shortening of the limb; shock.

Treatment

Immobilise the limb to prevent further injury and reduce the pain, using 'body' or improvised splints. Treat for shock. Place the patient on a stretcher in readiness to be taken to casualty or a ward. If possible, elevate the part slightly to reduce the swelling. To move the patient, spread a stretcher canvas under him and lift with poles.

Haemorrhage

Advanced malignant tumours often bleed freely from the whole surface. Erosion of a blood vessel may also occur, with dramatic results. Sudden and heavy blood loss may take place from tumours of the cervix uteri and the urinary bladder, though in the main bleeding from these organs is slow and continuous over a period of time, giving rise to anaemia.

Bleeding may take place from arteries, veins or capillary vessels. The source may be recognised by the way in which the blood issues from the wound and by its colour:

(1)   arterial bleeding – the blood is bright red and comes out in spurts;

(2)   venous bleeding – dark red blood in a continuous flow;

(3)   capillary bleeding – the blood oozes from the whole surface.

Treatment

Bleeding from a small wound or cut may be stopped by firm pressure over the site, unless there is a suspected underlying fracture. A cold compress, or holding the part under the cold tap, will also be effective. A firm dressing should be applied.

A major haemorrhage is an emergency situation for which the patient requires urgent medical attention and possible blood transfusion. Immediate steps must be taken to arrest the bleeding by application of firm pressure over the site, using a sterile pad held or bandaged in position. If bleeding is from an orifice, a sterile pack should be made available. Reassure and make the patient comfortable, try to conceal the blood as the sight will cause anxiety. The patient must be kept lying down and if possible the part elevated to reduce the pressure.

A patient who has lost a quantity of blood will exhibit signs of shock. There will be pallor with a cold clammy skin. The pulse rate will increase due to reduced blood volume. Breathing will be rapid or 'sighing' in an attempt to obtain more oxygen. The patient will become drowsy and restless.

Oxygen may be administered and the patient removed to the Casualty Department or to a ward with minimum delay.

Epistaxis (nose-bleeding) is common. The patient should be seated, leaning forwards with a bowl or tissues to collect the blood. Direct pressure to the nostril, and a cold compress, will help to stop the bleeding. He should be told to breathe through the mouth and discouraged from blowing the nose for fear of disturbing the clot which will form at the bleeding spot.

If bleeding is prolonged, medical advice must be sought. In the case of patients who have had large doses of radiation or chemotherapy a full blood count with platelet count should be requested.

Burns and scalds

Scalds are caused by moist heat – steam or boiling water. Burns are due to dry heat. In an electrical accident or an oxygen 'flash' burn, the area burned may be large. The features of both of these injuries are:
(a)   intense pain;
(b)   damage to the skin and possibly to underlying tissues also;
(c)   shock;
(d)   loss of serum from the injured areas contributes to this.

Treatment

Reduce the pain by application of cold moist sterile dressings. If the area is small it can be immersed in cold water. Lay the patient down and elevate the injured part if possible, to reduce fluid loss and swelling. Treat for shock. Constricting clothing and such objects as rings on burned fingers should be removed before swelling occurs, the skin around the area should be cleaned and sterile non-adherent dressings applied.

Head injury

Anyone who has received a blow on the head must not be allowed to leave the hospital until a doctor says that it is safe for him to do so. A blow on the head may cause:
(1)   Concussion – a disturbance or 'shaking' of the brain. It may or may not cause loss of consciousness. Concussion causes headache, nausea and vomiting and visual disturbance. These symptoms may last for several days after the accident. Concussion may also be delayed, the symptoms appearing several hours after the accident when the effects of bruising and oedema (swelling) make them apparent.
(2)   Fracture of the skull. This may be a simple crack in the bone which will unite in time. Alternatively a direct blow may push in part of the bone to cause pressure on the brain. In either case there will be internal bleeding which will raise the intracranial pressure. A fracture of the skull does not always cause loss of consciousness.

Treatment

If the patient is conscious and showing signs of concussion, lay him down to rest quietly and keep under observation until a doctor gives other instructions. Deal with any scalp wound. If the patient is unconscious, place him in the semi-prone position, remove any dentures and ease the jaw forward. Clear the mouth of vomit or saliva by swabbing or medical suction. Make a careful note of the patient's condition and level of consciousness and any change in these over the period of waiting for medical assistance – pulse, colour, type of respiration, signs of bleeding from the nose or ears, etc. Remove to the Accident and Emergency Department as soon as possible.

Injury to the eyes

If a foreign body cannot be easily removed from the eye, cover it with a sterile pad and take the patient to the Accident and Emergency Department. When drawing up fluids which are injurious to the tissues, such as cytotoxic drugs, eye-guards should be worn. Should such materials enter the eye, copious irrigation should be carried out immediately, using if necessary a running tap.

Shock

Shock is a term used to describe a reduction in the vital functions of the body due to fall in the systemic blood pressure. It accompanies many accidents, even minor ones.

Hypovolaemic shock describes actual loss of fluid by haemorrhage, serum loss or acute vomiting. It also includes internal bleeding at the site of an injury

Neurogenic shock may follow acute pain or severe emotional upset.

Anaphylactic shock is caused by circulatory collapse and may take place when foreign substances are injected intravenously. This reaction may occur with iodine compounds.

The degree of shock varies with the severity of the cause and to some extent from patient to patient. A mildly shocked patient will feel cold and sick and faint. There will be pallor of the skin and possibly vomiting.

Treatment

Lay the patient down and give comfort and reassurance. Treat the cause. Keep the patient under observation and report any signs of worsening of the condition.

In severe shock there will be loss or partial loss of consciousness. The skin will be pale, cold and moist. The pulse becomes rapid, but weak due to loss of blood volume and the breathing is shallow.

Treatment

Maintain a clear airway by turning the patient's head to one side and easing the jaw forward. Clear the mouth of obstructions. Alternatively, if there is vomiting, and other conditions allow, turn him semi-prone. Treat the cause. Oxygen may be given. Specialised medical care is urgent.

Administration of oxygen

Oxygen forms 20 per cent of the air. It is absorbed from air drawn into the lungs by haemoglobin and carried to the tissues where it is readily given up. Highly specialised tissue, such as the brain, cannot survive without oxygen and will suffer severe damage after a few minutes of deprivation. Less highly specialised tissue, such as muscles, can survive limited hypoxia (deprivation of oxygen).

Hypoxia occurs when:
(1)   disease of the lungs or blockage of the respiratory organs prevents oxygen being absorbed;
(2)   the nerve supply to the respiratory centres is affected;
(3)   there is a reduced volume of blood circulating due to disease of the circulatory system or an emergency situation such as shock or haemorrhage;
(4)   anemia is present.

Oxygenation of the tissues plays an important part in the response of tumours to radiotherapy. This is described in Chapter 7.

In the radiotherapy department there are two indications for administration of oxygen to patients:
(1)   respiratory distress due to a lung or intrathoracic tumour – a patient with a superior vena caval (S.V.C.) obstruction may be in extreme distress and require almost continuous oxygen;
(2)   in an accident situation, where there is shock or haemorrhage.

Oxygen is supplied by two methods:

(1)   In cylinders. The cylinders are coded black and white – a black cylinder with black and white shoulders. The cylinder is fitted with a pressure meter which records the amount in it in pounds per square inch (p.s.i.) and a flow meter which shows the amount of gas leaving the cylinder when the tap is opened. This is read in litres per minute. A key to open the cylinder is attached to the cylinder carriage and must not be removed. Cylinders must be checked daily.

(2)   In modern hospitals, oxygen is piped from a central supply to wards and departments.

Administration of oxygen for a short term is usually by disposable 'venti-mask'. These are made of plastic and have a malleable border to fit the face. They are perforated to allow the escape of expired gases. The procedure is to turn the oxygen supply full on to flood the mask, and the gas should be felt coming through before it is placed over the patient's face. The flow is then reduced to 3–5 litres per minute.

Supplied oxygen is dry, and if it is to be administered for any length of time it must be humidified or the patient will suffer discomfort from drying of the mucosa.

The B.L.B. mask has a 'rebreathing' bag attached in which the oxygen is warmed and moistened by the patient's exhaled breath. The oxygen may also be passed through a water bottle.

CARE OF THE UNCONSCIOUS PATIENT

The majority of unconscious patients encountered in the radiotherapy department are suffering from intracranial lesions (cerebral tumour or secondary disease in the brain). In these patients the general condition is stable and respiration is established. Some of these patients are very restless and disorientated.

(1)   They must have constant supervision while they are in the department.

(2)   Cot sides are essential on trolleys or beds and adequate support on the treatment couch.

(3)   Attention must be paid to comfort. They must not be left in a draught or placed too near a radiator. Packets of documents must not be placed on top of their limbs.

(4)   Lifting and handling must be done with care, and due attention paid to points of pressure and tubes (catheter or intravenous) attached to the body, so that they are not dragged or pulled out.

(5) It should be remembered that such patients are often able to hear and understand what is said, even though their motor functions are impaired.

Patients may also be sedated to enable treatment to be given. These are usually children, and sedation is arranged beforehand with the paediatrician. Close supervision is essential during the actual treatment and there should be secure support on the treatment couch. The medical officer remains nearby. After treatment the patient is placed on a trolley in the semi-prone position with the head low, and the trolley is removed to a screened cubicle. Constant supervision is essential until the patient regains consciousness, taking note of the colour, pulse and respiration.

NON-ACCIDENTAL EMERGENCIES

There are several emergency situations which can arise and which are not the result of an accident. These can occur at any time and the radiographer should be able to recognise them and know what to do.

Cardiac arrest

A cardiac arrest may occur as a result of a heart attack (coronary thrombosis). The coronary arteries supply the heart tissues. A thrombosis is a block caused by a blood clot. A heart attack may happen suddenly or the patient may have prior warning. The attack is preceded by acute pain in the left chest and behind the sternum. There may also be pain in the left arm and shoulder. The patient becomes confused, breathless and cyanosed (blue).

Treatment

If the patient is conscious, reassure and place in a semi-recumbent position. Call medical help. Give oxygen. Patients who suffer from angina (heart pain) carry tablets (glyceryl trinitrate) and the patient may be able to indicate that he has them. They are preventive rather than a treatment for the attack.

If the heart has stopped, this is a major emergency and specialised care must be initiated with minimum delay. Summon help on the emergency telephone number.

Signs

The patient will be unconscious, leaden in colour and often with froth (sometimes bloodstained) at the mouth. There will be no pulse. The pupils dilate and there is no response to light.

Treatment

Start resuscitation immediately – give the patient a sharp thump over the lower end of the sternum. This is called praecordial percussion and it may produce one or two heart beats. Start external cardiac massage. For this the patient must be on a flat firm surface such as the floor. Place the hands, one on top of the other on the chest, a little to the left of the sternum and, keeping the elbows straight, apply rhythmic pressure with the weight of the body behind it. The pressure must be sufficient to bend the ribs as it is meant to compress the heart. After five or six compressions, the lungs should be ventilated. There are several ways in which this may be done: In the absence of special equipment, direct mouth-to-mouth or mouth-to-nose expired air is used. The patient's mouth is held open by the operator's finger and cleaned by swabbing out. The operator takes a deep breath and, placing her mouth over that of the patient, expires air into it. The chest should be seen to expand as the air enters the lungs. Three or four breaths should be given before returning to massage.

It is no doubt distasteful to many people to think of placing one's mouth over that of the patient, but in a case of life or death this must take second place.

The Brook's Airway is kept in readiness in clinic and treatment rooms. This is a tube with a mouthpiece for the operator and an escape valve for expired air from the patient. The tube is passed into the back of the patient's throat while the tongue is pulled forward. Expired air is blown into the tube as in the mouth-to-mouth method.

The Ambu Bag is part of the equipment kept in the 'emergency box' in every department. This is an inflated bag with a face mask. The mask is fitted over the patient's face and held firmly in place by the operator gripping the mask and the patient's jaw, while at the same time pulling the jaw forward. As the bag is deflated by the other hand, air is forced into the lungs. Success depends on good contact between the mask and the face so that air does not escape round the edges.

Resuscitation should be continued until help arrives or the patient is pronounced dead by a doctor.

It is appropriate to mention that it is the deliberate policy in many radiotherapy departments to withhold cardiac resuscitation on patients with advanced malignant disease who have had a heart attack. This policy is indicated on the treatment sheet by the doctor in charge of the patient's treatment and he will indicate whether or not the patient is to be resuscitated should the need arise. This policy is not as callous as it may sound. A heart attack may bring speedy release to a patient nearing the end of his life, and spare him much suffering.

Fits and convulsions

In adults, fits and convulsions are associated with several conditions. Those most likely to be met with in the radiotherapy department include: (a) intracranial lesion – cerebral tumours and metastases; (b) epilepsy; (c) oxygen toxicity in a hyperbaric tank technique; (d) disturbance of the blood calcium in advanced malignant disease.

A patient who is subject to epileptic attacks has prior warning that he is about to have one. In other patients a feeling of unease or anxiety may precede the attack. When treating a patient in a hyperbaric tank it is important to look for signs. In a fit there are three stages:
(1)   Tonic – the patient becomes rigid with suspended respiration for about 30 seconds.
(2)   Clonic – there is twitching and jerking. Convulsive movements of the jaw may cause the tongue to be bitten. This lasts about a minute.
(3)   The patient becomes drowsy and may fall asleep. There may be incontinence of urine.

Management

During the clonic phase it is important to try to prevent the patient being injured. He must not be forcibly restrained. If he is on a couch the radiographer should stand beside the couch, place her arms across his body and hold the opposite side of the couch, making a 'bridge' over him. If the patient is on the floor it is possible to support his head on one's lap. Objects on which the patient may injure himself must be removed, and if there is a danger of the tongue being bitten a tongue depressor may be introduced at the side of the mouth and held between the teeth. When the fit is over a note of its duration and character should be made, and the patient made comfortable on a couch.

Diabetes and hypoglycaemia

Diabetes is a disorder of the metabolism arising from malfunction of the pancreas. Beta cells in the islelets of Langerhans, which secrete insulin, do not function, or do so only partially. Without insulin the body cannot metabolise sugar. This also causes changes in the metabolism of proteins and fats and in the blood chemistry. Cytotoxic drugs may precipitate the condition. Many diabetic patients require regular injections of insulin. All require a carefully regulated diet. Most either wear a Medic-Alert bracelet or carry a card. There are two emergency situations which may arise:

(1) The patient has had insufficient insulin. This is unlikely to occur in the radiotherapy department. It occurs if a patient is ill and unable to tell anyone he is diabetic, or if the fact is not discovered. The patient becomes faint and dizzy and acetone can be smelt on his breath (ketosis).

(2) Hypoglycaemia (low blood sugar). The patient has had too little to eat or is in need of a meal. This also occurs as a result of vomiting, or of increased metabolism due to unaccustomed exertion. It may occur in the radiotherapy department where patients often wait for transport home, or for the results of blood tests if the waiting period is long and extends over a meal-time.

Reactions to radiation and to drugs, which affect the patient's appetite, are also contributory.

Signs

The patient becomes confused and giddy. He may become aggressive. The state has sometimes been mistaken for drunkenness. There is visual disturbance and paraesthesia (loss of feeling). The patient is sweating and clammy but not dehydrated.

Treatment

The patient must be given a sweet drink or something sweet to eat; many carry sugar for this purpose. When arranging appointments for diabetic patients this need must be considered, and when a patient is likely to be in the department or hospital over a meal-time some form of refreshment must be available. This applies to non-diabetics as well as diabetics. Hospitals have coffee bars, but it is not unknown for a patient arriving by ambulance to have no money! When required, a meal can be arranged for a patient in a ward.

Electric shock

In any department using electrical equipment, all personnel must be familiar with the location of the main switches. In the case of electric shock two situations arise:

(1) The current passing through the body causes the muscles to go into spasm. The victim cannot let go of the source and is electrocuted.

(2) With alternating current the victim is thrown off the source, often with considerable force, and the injuries may include burns, bruising and even fracture.

Procedure

(1) Isolate the main switch. Do not touch the victim while the source is live.

(2) Look for signs of cardiac arrest and treat immediately.

(3) If the patient is conscious, treat for shock.

(4) Treat the other injuries.

Fire

In departments with electrical equipment there is the risk of fire. This is minimised by proper care and maintenance of the machinery.

   The use of oxygen and anaesthetic gases in radiotherapy treatment rooms carries a certain amount of risk because of the possibility of electrical sparking. Cobalt 60 units are preferred for safety in these techniques. All personnel must be familiar with the location of fire extinguishers and with the procedures to be followed in the case of fire. These are: sound the alarm; isolate the main switches; close the doors and windows to reduce the air; fire doors should be kept closed at all times; evacuate patients and personnel. Most deaths are due to fumes and smoke. If the fire is controllable, use an extinguisher. Do not use water on an electrical fire. Inform the Radiation Protection Officer. If the fire brigade is called, inform the senior officer if there are radioactive materials in the area.

Chapter 4
Hygiene and Cross-infection in the Radiotherapy Department

Cross-infection is the acquisition of a disease by contact with a source of infection. Hospitals are full of people who are ill, and some of them have infectious conditions. People who are ill have a lowered resistance to disease and are therefore much more at risk. The very extensive use of bactericidal substances, especially antibiotics, has produced strains of bacteria which are resistant, and this complicates the picture. When one considers the numbers of patients treated in hospitals every day throughout the country, it will be seen that when news of an outbreak of infection in one of them reaches the newspapers, it is an unusual occurrence, but it is only by constant vigilance that this standard is maintained.

CAUSES OF DISEASE

Disease is caused by several agents: (1) bacteria; (2) viruses; (3) parasites; (4) fungi.

Bacteria

Bacteria are small unicellular organisms which may be seen with the aid of a microscope of suitable magnification. They are plant micro-organisms. There are many thousands of bacteria present all the time, though not all are harmful. Many are beneficial and even necessary to health; for instance the soil bacteria which fix nitrogen and the protective 'flora' of the mouth. Bacteria which are harmful are called pathogens. They multiply in the tissues and produce toxins (poisons) and other effects which cause illness. The different types of bacteria are divided into three main groups:

Coccoid (sing. coccus; pl. cocci)

These are small round organisms. These again are divided into three groups according to the way in which they group themselves.

45

(1)   Staphylococci – are seen in groups like bunches of grapes. They are mainly pus-forming – sepsis, boils etc., and there are many varieties.

(2)   Streptococci – form chains like strings of beads. They are found in the throat and upper respiratory tract in acute infections such as scarlet fever and tonsilitis.

(3)   Diplococci – these organisms join in pairs. They are the organisms of some forms of pneumonia, meningitis and gonorrhoea.

Bacilli (Bacillus)

These are rod-shaped organisms. Some of them have whip-like attachments (flagellae) by which they swim in the body fluids.

Vibrios and Spirillae

These are curved or spiral organisms. They include organisms causing gastrointestinal infections and spirochaetes.

Bacterial growth

Bacteria are living organisms and need the correct conditions for growth and reproduction. They need food, moisture and warmth. Some organisms are aerobic, i.e. they need oxygen. Others need the absence of oxygen and these are called anaerobic. Some are facultative – they can live with or without oxygen. Certain bacteria require an acid or an alkaline environment and some are specific to certain tissues of the body. For instance *Escherichia coli*, which lives in the bowel and is necessary for the production of vitamin B, will cause very unpleasant infections if it enters the urinary tract or an open wound.

Bacterial infections can be controlled by depriving the bacteria of the conditions needed for life. Spore-forming bacteria are bacteria which can survive for very long periods in a dormant state until the environment becomes suitable for growth. These organisms change their bodies and grow a protective coat when conditions become unsuitable. Spores are rather like the seed of a plant. They are very resistant to heat and cold and to disinfectants which cannot dissolve the protective coat. Pulmonary tuberculosis is caused by a spore-forming organism.

Viruses

Viruses are smaller than bacteria and can only be seen with an electron microscope. Like bacteria, viruses may be harmless or pathogenic. Their action in the tissues is different from that of bacteria. They invade and multiply in the cells of the body.

Fungi

Fungi are vegetable organisms and some species invade animal tissues and cause disease. The fungus grows in the tissues putting out masses of strands called mycelia. Fruiting bodies are formed, filled with reproductive spores. These spores are released and easily disseminate in the air. Fungus diseases occurring in humans include ringworm (tinea), monilia (a skin infection) and thrush. Thrush is an infection of the mucosa caused by *Candida albicans*. It is an infection to which patients who are receiving radiotherapy for a lesion in the mouth or throat are particularly prone unless strict oral hygiene is observed. Radiation destroys the natural protective flora of the mouth, allowing the infection to take hold. It causes the patient a great deal of discomfort and, when combined with the effects of the radiation, a great deal of tissue damage.

Parasites

Parasites live at the expense of their host. They may be simple unicellular organisms such as amoeba or protozoa, or they may be complex creatures – an insect such as a louse or a flea. Parasites can cause illness in the host by simply upsetting its well-being and comfort. They can also carry disease which is introduced into the tissues of the host through bites. The host may suffer malnutrition as a result, and become more prone to other diseases. Some parasites are a contributing factor to other unrelated diseases in that they irritate the tissues and cause changes to take place. For example, the parasite *Bilharzia*, which is found in rivers in the Middle East, is a contributing factor to tumours of the urinary bladder. The parasite enters the urinary tract and irritates the bladder wall.

THE DEFENCE MECHANISMS OF THE BODY

Resistance to disease is due to the defence mechanisms of the body which deal with incoming infective organisms and neutralise them before they can take effect. These defences include the lymphatic system and the white cells (leukocytes) in the blood which originate in the lymphatic system and in the bone marrow. In the case of infection, the white cells attempt to control the invading organisms by phagocytic action. Phagocytes are irregularly shaped cells which engulf and destroy the pathogenic organisms. The presence of a bacterial infection stimulates the production of phagocytes and increases the number of white cells in the blood. In the case of a viral infection, many of these cells are destroyed by the action of the viruses. A viral infection can in fact decrease the white cell count in the blood and therefore lower the patient's resistance to illness.

Irradiation of parts of the body containing haemopoietic (blood cell-producing) tissue, and the use of certain cytotoxic drugs, inhibits the production of white cells. This removes some of the body's protection and makes the patient more prone to infectious illnesses. Patients undergoing a course of radiotherapy should try to avoid coming into contact with infectious conditions, in particular those caused by viruses. Virus conditions include the common cold, influenza, measles and chickenpox.

THE IMMUNE RESPONSE

An important line of defence in the body is the formation of antibodies by some of the white cells. The presence of a bacterial infection stimulates the production of antibodies to combat it. In some cases the incubation period of the disease is shorter than the time needed for the formation of antibodies. If this is so, the disease will make its appearance in the patient. In other cases the antibodies will be mobilised quickly and the disease will be resisted. In this case the patient is said to be immune. Immunity to some diseases is inherited. A baby receives some protection from its mother. Further immunity is acquired by coming into contact with, or having had, an infection and recovering. With some infections, immunity is lifelong.

Immunity may also be acquired artificially by means of vaccination or inoculation with a vaccine or serum prepared from a dead organism. This type of immunity is used to prevent epidemics of serious diseases such as diphtheria, or to give protection against lethal infections such as smallpox when the resistance of the population is low.

If a very large volume of the body is irradiated, the immune response may be considerably reduced and the patient will have very little resistance to infection. He will be in a critical state and require special nursing care (reverse barrier nursing). This condition may be deliberately brought about by 'total body irradiation' prior to a bone-marrow transplant. The immune response is removed so that the body will not reject the foreign marrow implanted into it. A radiation accident, or exposure to atomic fallout, could cause the same conditions.

REVERSE BARRIER NURSING

This is a special nursing technique designed to protect a patient from infections when he has little or no resistance. The indications for it are based on the neutrophil count rather than the total white cell count. A patient with a neutrophil count of less than 1000 per ml is at risk. In reversed barrier nursing the patient is virtually isolated, and this may cause him some stress. It is also very demanding of nursing resources, as one or more nurses are totally committed to the care of one patient. Reverse barrier nursing entails:

(1) strict daily attention to the patient's person and environment;
(2) gowning up of all personnel entering his room;
(3) sterilising of all equipment to be used on or by the patient, including eating utensils and cutlery;
(4) careful selection and preparation of all food and drink to ensure that it is bacteria-free.

When total body irradiation is to be carried out the treatment room must be prepared beforehand to eliminate, as far as possible, the risk of the patient contracting any infection. Preparation includes swabbing all equipment with a mild antiseptic solution and changing all the linen. Any member of the staff who has a cold or throat infection is excluded during the procedure.

ROUTES OF INFECTION

The Health and Safety at Work Act requires that working conditions should be hygienic as well as safe. Hygienic conditions include such basic conditions as proper lighting, heating, ventilation and adequate toilet facilities. There should be enough space for the occupants to move about and work in comfort and safety. It should also preferably be attractive in appearance to give a sense of satisfaction and well-being. These conditions are essential in any large public building, and in a hospital, where many of the users are sick, the need is even greater.

In a hospital it is important to be aware of the possibility of cross-infection. General hospitals do not deliberately admit patients with infectious diseases – they are sent to isolation hospitals which have special facilities for nursing them – but there is always the possibility that one may be admitted and the condition not diagnosed until he is in the ward or department. There are also instances when a condition of bio-hazard may exist. This is a situation where the risk of infection is very high – usually in laboratories where specimens are handled – but it could arise in other situations.

Infection may enter the body by three main routes:
(1) inhalation: breathing in the infective organism in the air;
(2) ingestion: swallowing infected food or drink;
(3) inoculation: the infection enters the tissues through damaged skin or via the mucosal surfaces.

Inhalation

Most airborne bacteria are trapped on the moist surfaces of the respiratory tract and destroyed by the natural flora of the mouth. The lymphatic tissues – of which there is a rich supply in the upper respiratory passages – are also protective. When the mucosal surfaces are damaged or inflamed the protection is greatly reduced.

Radiation treatment causes an inflammatory reaction in mucosa subjected to it. A high dose of radiation also destroys the natural protective flora. For these reasons, patients who are undergoing a course of treatment to a lesion of the mouth, throat or chest are advised to avoid places where they are likely to come into contact with airborne infections (buses, trains, places of entertainment and crowds generally) and are often brought to the hospital by ambulance or hospital car service.

Dust is dangerous in that it may carry spores, particularly those of respiratory diseases such as tuberculosis. Modern hospitals are constructed to eliminate dust traps, and have sealed floors and washable surfaces. Damp dusting and suction cleaning remove dust, and do not just move it from place to place. Good air-conditioning reduces airborne bacteria by filtering the incoming air and maintaining constant circulation. A major source of bacteria in the air is soiled linen and outdoor clothing. This is one of the reasons for asking patients to change in a cubicle. Apart from time-saving and privacy, it reduces the risk of bringing infective organisms into the treatment room. Disposable couch covers and washable cotton covers on sand and bolus bags help to maintain treatment room hygiene.

Protective clothing in the form of washable uniforms and white coats is worn by personnel in the clinical areas of the hospital. To serve its purpose, it should be changed regularly, or it will be no protection either to the wearer or to the patient with whom she is dealing.

Masks which are worn for aseptic procedures may also be a major source of infection. The interior of the mask becomes warm and damp, creating the perfect conditions for bacterial growth. A mask kept hanging round the neck after the task is finished will quickly become a source of danger rather than a protection.

Waterproof dressing bags are provided for the disposal of soiled dressings. Dressings should be put into them as soon as they are removed from the patient, and the bag closed. Pus and discharge can disseminate staphylococci into the air as they dry. A bad outbreak of sepsis among patients whose resistance is low can be difficult to control.

In a department where people come into contact with each other, it is impossible to avoid colds, particularly in winter. In a radiotherapy department many patients are very susceptible to infection and members of the staff who are unfortunate enough to have coughs and sneezes should try not to pass them on. While not encouraging absenteeism, it is sometimes better to get the worst of the cold over at home.

Ingestion

Infection may enter the alimentary tract in food and drink. This may be due to dirty hands, contaminated food or utensils. Most of these infections are waterborne gastrointestinal infections. Proper washing facilities and efficient cleaning of possible sites of infection are essential.

In hospital departments the 'clean utility' and 'dirty utility' areas are separate. The clean utility is used for the preparation of clean trolleys, drawing up drugs and the storage of sterile equipment. The dirty area is used for the disposal of used equipment and for any task where there is a risk of bacterial infection.

A possible source of infection in both the X-ray and radiotherapy department is the darkroom. The darkroom is warm and damp, and frequently not very well ventilated. It creates the perfect conditions for bacterial growth. A clean darkroom is essential for good standards of work. It is also essential for good health.

Inoculation

All surgical procedures, dressings and injections are carried out under aseptic conditions. Asepsis means the exclusion of all micro-organisms.

The C.S.S.D. (Central Sterile Services Department) in the hospital prepares all the sterile dressing and theatre packs. These packs contain the necessary instruments and dressings for particular procedures and they are sterilised after packing by autoclaving. In the C.S.S.D. very strict controls are exercised as regards the efficiency of the sterilising procedure. Many items of equipment, including catheters, hypodermic needles and syringes are supplied to the hospital by commercial firms, pre-packed and sterile.

Healthy skin and mucosa act as barriers to infection. If these surfaces are damaged the barrier is not as efficient. A radiation reaction at the site of the treatment is a form of damage, and with it there is an increased risk of infection. The patient's personal hygiene is of vital importance during a course of radiotherapy and it is a matter in which the radiographer must take an active interest. The reactions of the various tissues, with their care and treatment, are fully described in later chapters.

Another potential source of damage to the skin are used needles and scalpel blades. These can carry very serious infections including hepatitis, and any injury sustained from them must be reported immediately. Special cardboard boxes are supplied for their safe disposal. They must never be put into a dressing disposal bag from which they can protrude to injure a member of the staff.

TREATMENT OF INFECTIONS

Prior to starting a course of radiotherapy, steps are taken to eliminate any infection in the area to be irradiated. Infection reduces the tolerance of tissue to radiation by devitalising it and impairing the ability of the normal cells to recover. When sepsis is allowed to continue unchecked in an irradiated zone, necrosis (death of tissue) may occur.

Secondly, during a course of radiation treatment, a reaction on a mucosal surface may be exacerbated by an infection which was not present when the course was begun. This is something for which the radiographer must be constantly vigilant.

Infection may also reduce the effect of radiation on the tumour. Pus and necrotic tissue in the tumour area may cause a reduction of the blood supply to the tumour and the tumour cells will therefore be hypoxic (poorly supplied with oxygen). Hypoxic cells are more resistant to radiation than those supplied with oxygen (oxic) and the effect of the treatment will be diminished. The presence of oxygen is necessary for radiation to be effective.

Infections are treated with a suitable antibiotic once the nature of the infection and its sensitivity have been established. For this a sample of the infected material is obtained from the patient and sent to the laboratory for bacteriological examination.

COLLECTIONS OF SPECIMENS

Infected wounds and mucosal surfaces

When the infected area is a wound containing pus or an infected mucosal surface, a specimen is obtained on a sterile swab. The swab is composed of cotton wool attached to a stick, the other end of which is inserted into a cork. The stick and the swab are enclosed in a sterile tube and the cork closes the end of the tube. A specimen of the material must be obtained before the wound is cleaned or any anti-bacteriological agent applied. Holding the stick by means of the cork, it is withdrawn from the tube, care being taken not to touch any other part. The swab is dipped in the pus or wiped over the infected surface, and then carefully replaced in the tube.

Sputum

Sputum is collected by asking the patient to cough it into a screw-topped plastic jar. If the patient has difficulty in producing sputum during the day, he may be given the jar to take home because patients with productive coughs usually produce more on rising in the morning than they do later. In this case it must be impressed on the patient that the specimen be brought to the hospital as soon as possible after its collection, and that it be kept in a cool place because many bacteria have a short life away from their host.

Urine

Urine is also collected in a sterile screw-top jar by asking the patient to pass it into a sterile measure and then pouring it into the jar. In most cases a C.V.S.U. (clean voided specimen of urine) is sufficient.

If a catheter specimen is required, this must be obtained in the ward or in Casualty, as it is an aseptic procedure.

To obtain a C.V.S.U. the urethral orifice must be cleaned with sterile water before the urine is passed. An antiseptic solution should not be used in case some of it mixes with the urine and inhibits the growth of any bacteria which may be present. Patients naturally prefer to do this for themselves in privacy, but careful instructions must be given as to what is required. A sterile tray for this purpose is obtainable from the C.S.S.D. containing the following items:

(1)   a paper towel;
(2)   a small gallipot to hold sterile water;
(3)   swabs to clean the area;
(4)   a measure or bowl to receive the specimen.

Also required are:

(1)   sterile water in the gallipot;
(2)   a disposable bag for the used swabs;
(3)   a specimen pot, labelled with the patient's data and a request form for the laboratory.

The patient is given the following instructions:

(1)   remove clothing;
(2)   wash the hands and dry them on the towel;
(3)   clean the area, using each swab once only and discarding it;
(4)   pass a specimen of urine into the bowl or measure, taking care to handle only the outside of the utensil.

When the patient is male, he should be asked to pass some urine into the lavatory pan before passing the specimen into the bowl. By doing so, the urethra will be washed free of bacteria and any remaining will probably be from the bladder itself.

Urine decomposes very rapidly if left for any length of time, so the specimen should be sent to the laboratory without delay.

THE SPECIMEN REFRIGERATOR

Specimens may have to be kept in the department for some time before they can be sent to the laboratory. In this case they must be kept in a cool place. This slows decomposition and bacterial growth and lengthens the life of the bacteria which may be present. A specimen refrigerator is provided for this purpose. This is located in the dirty utility area. Specimen containers should be put into plastic bags before being put into the refrigerator to lessen the risk of cross-contamination. This refrigerator must on no account be used for any other purpose as it is a potential bio-hazard.

LABELLING OF SPECIMENS

Specimen containers must be labelled clearly before being sent to the laboratory with the patient's identification data, type of specimen and date. The time at which the specimen was obtained must be stated, as some bacteria have a limited life. If the patient is already taking an antibiotic, this must also be stated as it can make a difference to the sensitivity of the specimen. The specimen is sent to the laboratory with a request for culture and sensitivity.

CULTURE AND SENSITIVITY OF BACTERIA

This request means that the doctor wants to know:
(1) Are there any pathogens in the specimen?
(2) What kind of organisms are they?
(3) Which antibiotic will kill them?
In the laboratory a sample of the material is incubated (cultured) on a suitable nutrient jelly such as agar in order to encourage bacterial growth. A slide is prepared from the growth in order to identify the organism under the microscope. Antibiotics are applied to the growth on the jelly to determine which will kill it.

GRAM-POSITIVE AND GRAM-NEGATIVE BACTERIA

This is a method of classifying bacteria and therefore making the task of identification easier. It takes its name from a Danish physician who devised a method of staining slides. Some bacteria take up the stain and these are called Gram-positive. Others which do not take up the stain are called Gram-negative. When a diagnosis has to be made, the number of possibilities is reduced by elimination. Bacteriological reports take about a week to come from the laboratory and the patient will usually have begun an antibiotic treatment before it is received. The report which will be returned to the department will be something like the following:
  The specimen showed a Gram+ staphylococcus:
    Sensitive to penicillin
    Resistant to terramycin

METHODS OF STERILISING EQUIPMENT

It is of help to the student to know the various methods by which equipment is made sterile in the hospital, and to know the advantages and disadvantages of each method. Certain items will be damaged by being sterilised by the wrong method. In other cases, the process of sterilisation will be ineffective if it is not carried out properly. The purpose of sterilising materials is to destroy all micro-organisms.

Heat

Wet heat – boiling

This is not 100 per cent safe, and is certainly not effective against spores because they can resist the temperature of boiling water. The temperature can be raised by 1 or 2 degrees by adding a small quantity of a chemical (e.g. sodium bicarbonate) to the water and this will make it more effective. The water itself must be boiled for 5 minutes to sterilise it before adding the articles. Boiling is not used in hospitals as a means of sterilising.

Dry heat

Baking at 150° for ½ hour will destroy bacteria. This method is used for infected linen and for medicaments like Vaseline gauze.

Autoclaving

The autoclave combines both heat, in the form of steam, and pressure. It is a very efficient method, and is used in hospitals for the preparation of theatre packs, dressings and many instruments. It has some disadvantages in that some materials are damaged by it – some plastics and rubber – and therefore cannot be sterilised by this method. A brief description of the method is as follows:
(1)   The prepared packs are put into a sealed cylinder.
(2)   The air is evacuated.
(3)   Superheated steam is then pumped in to a given pressure (from 20 to 40 lb/in²)and this pressure is maintained for a given time (20–30 min).
(4)   The cylinder is then evacuated again. The vacuum created will dry the contents by evaporating all the moisture.

(5) Cold sterile air is then admitted to equalise the pressure and permit the cylinder to be opened.

(6) Continuous monitoring of the system is carried out by including a chemical device which changes colour when subjected to heat and pressure.

(7) The sterilised packs are dated and coded. Outdated packs should not be used as their sterility will not be guaranteed.

Chemical

Chemical sterilising is used in a large variety of situations. It is important to ensure that articles to be sterilised by a chemical are clean so that the sterilising agent can reach the surface. It is also important to know the time required for the chemical to be effective. Needless to say, the chemical should not be damaging to the item to be sterilised, although some plastics and cements are gradually eroded and damaged by repeated sterilising.

Examples of situations in which chemical sterilisation is used are as follows:

(1) When an object will be damaged by heat. Lead internal eye-shields are sterilised in hibitane for 5 min.

(2) Antiseptic solutions are used to clean the skin before surgery, to clean wounds before dressing them and to clean the hands before carrying out an aseptic procedure.

(3) Antibiotics and other drugs are used to kill bacteria in the body.

(4) Sites of possible infection, e.g. sinks, drains, sluices, etc., are rendered safe by chemical disinfectants.

(5) Chemical gases such as formalin may be used in a fume cupboard to sterilise objects which have been infected by an infectious illness, e.g. children's toys in the ward.

Radiation

(1) Infrared radiation – dry heat is of course infrared radiation.

(2) Ultraviolet – U.V. light is bacteriological and anaerobic bacteria are destroyed by sunlight. Ultraviolet radiation is used in the physiotherapy department to inhibit persistent infections. It has been used to sterilise water in swimming pools and to prevent the spread of infection between beds in wards. It has considerable disadvantages however. U.V. light will cause eye damage if dark glasses are not worn. It will also damage the skin with prolonged exposure, and it is carcinogenic.

(3) Gamma radiation – gamma radiation is bactericidal if a sufficiently high dose is given. $2\frac{1}{2}$ million cGy is required to ensure safety. Sterilisation by this means is commercially carried out, and equipment such as syringes, hypodermic needles, catheters and other disposable items are pre-packed in sealed containers and irradiated. The radiation source is cobalt 60.

TRAYS AND TROLLEYS FOR ASEPTIC PROCEDURE

The preparation of many aseptic procedures is greatly simplified nowadays by the use of individual packs, made up by the C.S.S.D., containing the necessary items. A second advantage of this system is that it is much safer. The risk of inadequate cleaning and sterilising of instruments is eliminated. Many of the instruments supplied are disposable. Those that are re-usable are returned to the C.S.S.D. after use.

The disadvantages of the system are:
(1)   it is quite costly, though this must be weighed against patient safety;
(2)   it adds to the already impressive volume of disposable rubbish we have to cope with in every situation of life.
A pack, on average, is composed as follows:
(1)   it includes a plastic tray with dressings and instruments, and a gallipot or compartment for lotions;
(2)   it is wrapped in a waterproof sheet which, when opened out, forms a sterile working surface.
(3)   the whole is sealed in a paper bag which can be used for rubbish when the pack is used.

For technical reasons it is impossible for a pack to contain everything that is needed for a specific procedure, and when anything more complicated than a simple dressing is to be done a sterile trolley is prepared.

PREPARATION OF A STERILE TROLLEY

Sterile trolleys are prepared in the clean utility area of the department. A dressing trolley has an upper and a lower shelf which, for reasons of hygiene, are made of metal or glass. The upper shelf is the sterile working surface, the lower shelf carries the non-sterile items which are needed during the procedure.

Before the trolley is laid, the shelves are cleaned by washing them and wiping them with a mild antiseptic. The bars under the edges of the shelves must also be cleaned.

The lower shelf is prepared first. The logic of this should be obvious. By bending down to clean or lay the lower shelf, the upper one may be touched or breathed on, and so contaminated. Once the lower shelf has been cleaned and laid, the upper shelf is prepared. The sterile pack is removed from its bag and placed on the clean surface. The paper sheet enclosing the items is not unwrapped until immediately before the procedure is carried out.

A matter of great anxiety to many students is trying to memorise the items to put on a trolley for each procedure. This need not be difficult if the student takes care to watch carefully while the procedure is being carried out, and to assist with it. It is then possible to go over the steps of the procedure mentally while preparing the trolley. In this way, no item will be overlooked, and it is a more intelligent method than trying to memorise a list.

INFECTIONS OF SPECIAL SIGNIFICANCE

Pulmonary tuberculosis (T.B.)

This is occasionally encountered among patients attending the radiotherapy department, not necessarily in connection with a lung tumour. Although it presents a risk, especially to younger members of the staff, the risk is not as great as it once was. This is because:

(1) new antibiotics are available to bring the disease under control quickly;

(2) it is only rarely that a patient will reach the department with the condition undetected. Unless radiotherapy is urgently needed, an open infection will be treated first.

Pulmonary tuberculosis is spread via the expectorate from the lungs – droplet infection – dried sputum on the hands, clothes or handkerchief, etc. The infective organism is spore-forming and has a long spore life.

When a patient has been cured of tuberculosis the lesions in the lungs calcify. Irradiation of the lungs may reactivate the disease, hence if a patient has had T.B. in the past, and is to undergo treatment to the chest, anti-tuberculosis drugs are given as a precautionary measure.

If a patient is known to have an open (active) infection, some precautions need to be taken to protect the staff, but the patient must never be made to feel that he is a 'leper' or even of special interest. The following rules should be followed:

(1)   The staff treating him should be informed in advance of the infection so that preparations may be made in the treatment room.

(2)   To cut down the risk of cross-infection, as few people as possible should be involved in the treatment.

(3)   The patient should be treated at the end of the day or at the end of the morning session so that the room can be well ventilated before another patient enters it. This also gives time for cleaning and changing the linen.

(4)   There must be strict attention to hygiene in the room. Disposable covers should be used on the couch and any drinking utensils used by the patient, and any tissues, etc., treated as being infected. Any item of equipment used in or near the mouth must be disinfected.

As a general rule, younger people are more susceptible to T.B. and the degree of susceptibility is assessed by a Mantoux test. This is a pre-training requirement for all radiography students.

Herpes zoster

Another condition, which manifests itself by a skin eruption, is herpes zoster (shingles). This is a viral infection which appears to have a connection with malignant disease and with radiotherapy. The virus irritates a nerve root ganglion and the blistered rash appears along the track of the nerve affected. It also causes considerable pain along the nerve track and the patient feels generally unwell. Herpes is mildly infectious and should be treated as such. The most common site is the mid-dorsal, with the rash extending round to the front of the chest. A more serious site is that of the trigeminal nerve, when the rash may extend across the eye and damage the cornea.

In the early stages of the infection, when blisters are present, local application of idoxuridine 5 per cent with dimethyl sulphoxide to 100 per cent solution may relieve the pain, but in some older patients the pain may be intractable, giving rise to considerable distress. This pain is called post-herpetic neuralgia. It sometimes responds to small doses of radiation, but may have to be treated by nerve block.

Chapter 5
Drugs in Radiotherapy and Oncology

A drug is a substance which produces an effect in the tissues. Drugs are used to treat disease, to prevent an illness and to relieve symptoms. Strictly speaking, X-ray contrast media are not drugs, but for practical purposes they are included under the heading.

All drugs are dangerous if misused, and in certain cases give rise to social problems. Regulations relating to their availability, and the duties and responsibilities of professional personnel who have dealings with them, are the subject of an Act of Parliament.

The Pharmacy and Poisons Act 1933 restricted the supply, use and labelling of poisons and drugs. It also provided for a number of Schedules into which drugs are classified. The Drugs Acts of 1964, 1965 and 1967 established greater control of 'dangerous' drugs and their availability. The Misuse of Drugs Act 1971 replaced these Acts. This Act gives tighter control over certain drugs and enables and requires the Home Secretary and the Secretary of State for Scotland to make further Regulations as required.

SCHEDULES

Only two of the four schedules need to be considered as far as the radiographer is concerned:

Schedule 1. Includes drugs which may be purchased by the general public under certain conditions. These are substances such as aspirin, some cough mixtures, etc., which are sold by a chemist (or pharmacist). The drug must be named on the label, together with the strength of the mixture or tablets and the recommended dose. The drugs in this schedule are exempt from many of the controls applied to the other schedules.

Schedule 2. These drugs are only obtainable on written prescription from a doctor, dental practitioner or veterinary surgeon. They include the 'dangerous' or habit-forming drugs such as cocaine and morphine. The schedule also covers hormones, sedatives and many preparations which contain controlled drugs. Controlled drugs, which are often referred to as D.D.A. (Dangerous Drugs Act) drugs, are subject to strict regulations as regards storage, prescribing and administering.

STORAGE

The drug cupboard

Drugs and medicines are kept in a locked cupboard. The cupboard must be made of metal and be fastened to the wall. A red warning light on the cupboard illuminates when the door is opened. The key is in the charge of a qualified nurse.

The drug refrigerator

Some drugs deteriorate if they are stored in a warm place. Certain cytotoxic (cell-poisoning) drugs and some antibiotics must be stored in cool conditions. The drug refrigerator is exactly like a domestic one, except that it is locked. It is subject to the same conditions as the drug cupboard. This refrigerator must never be used to store food. There is a risk that bacteria will be introduced in the food or the wrappings to contaminate the drugs. There is also the risk that spillage of a drug will contaminate the food.

DEPARTMENTAL RECORDS

The senior nursing officer of the department is responsible for ensuring that a correct stock of the necessary drugs is maintained. The amount held is shown in the drug book. When a controlled drug is administered to a patient in the department, the particulars must be recorded in the record book in ink, and the entry signed.

PATIENT PRESCRIPTIONS

Only a qualified practitioner may prescribe a drug. The prescription is written on a prescription sheet for the hospital pharmacy, or on a form which may be taken to a dispensing chemist. Before the prescription is written, the patient's name, address and hospital number must be entered on the form. This is a precaution against it being improperly used. When the prescription is a repeat of a previous one, the date and the quantity of the drug prescribed on the earlier occasions must be checked to ensure that an excessive amount is not being obtained. As a rule, patients do not try to get more than they need, but there are instances of attempted suicide and addiction.

UNITS OF MEASUREMENT

All drugs are supplied in metric units. In solid form, i.e. tablets or pills, there is a stated number of milligrams (mg) of drug per tablet or pill. In liquid form there is a stated number of mg per millilitre (ml) of fluid. The drug is prescribed in mg. The number of tablets or pills, or the amount of liquid, can be calculated.

LABELLING

All drug containers must be labelled. The label must state:
(1)   the name of the drug and the total quantity in the bottle;
(2)   the strength in mg per tablet, or ml;
(3)   the dose and the intervals at which it is to be taken;
(4)   the name of the patient for whom it is prescribed.
   In the case of stock bottles kept in the department, the bottle is labelled 'Stock' and the name of the department. In any case where the label is illegible, the container must be returned to the pharmacy.

Before administration to the patient

(1)   check that the correct dose is being given.
(2)   check that the correct drug is being administered.
(3)   check that the correct patient is receiving it.
Controlled drugs must be checked by a second qualified person, who must also sign the book.

Routine checking of drug stocks
(carried out daily)

(1)   The quantity held is checked against the stock book.
(2)   Empty or nearly-empty containers are returned to the pharmacy.
(3)   On no account may the contents of one container be emptied into another.

(4) The date of expiry is checked, and out-of-date drugs returned to the pharmacy.

(5) Check that there is an adequate amount of sterile fluids for making up and diluting drugs.

(6) The drug refrigerator is checked to ensure that it is clean, operating at the correct temperature and does not need defrosting.

DRUGS USED IN RADIOTHERAPY AND ONCOLOGY

The use of drugs as a method of treatment is called chemotherapy. For some forms of malignant disease, chemotherapy is the treatment of choice. In other cases drugs are used to assist or enhance the effect of radiation. Many of the drugs have marked side-effects, some of which may be permanent. This is an accepted hazard and their administration is only carried out under close medical supervision.

Hormones and steroids

These are substances which are produced by the ductless glands of the body, though some hormone preparations are manufactured synthetically. These substances affect the behaviour of different organs and glands, and alter the growth of some tumours.

(1) Oestrogens are ovarian hormones. They are used mainly in the treatment of tumours of the breast and of the prostate.

(2) Progesterones are also ovarian hormones. They are used in the treatment of breast, renal and endometrial tumours.

(3) Androgens are testicular hormones and used mainly in the treatment of tumours of the female breast.

(4) Corticosteroids are produced by the adrenal cortex. These are also used in the treatment of breast tumours, but corticosteroids have many uses in medicine for the treatment of non-malignant as well as malignant conditions.

The side-effects of hormones and steroids, when used as a method of treatment include weight gaining and possibly fluid retention.

Patients on steroid treatment must be kept under close medical supervision and must carry a blue 'steroid' card, in case of any untoward accident which needs medical treatment. Any other doctor or dentist must be informed that the patient is receiving steroids before other drugs are given or any operation performed. The consequence of overlooking this could be serious. When corticosteroids are given for any length of time, the patient's own secretions are reduced. This in turn affects other ductless glands, part of whose function is to help the body adjust to states of stress.

Antibiotics

Antibiotics are given to treat infections prior to treatment, but powerful antibiotics also assist the action of the radiation by preventing the recovery of damaged cells. Bleomycin is given by injection 20 min before irradiation. Other antibiotics include actinomycin D and daunomycin. These are also damaging to normal tissue.

Drugs affecting cell growth

These are a group of highly toxic drugs which are taken up selectively by growing cells and which poison the cells or interfere in various ways with their metabolism to prevent them dividing. They are sometimes called cytotoxic (cell-poisoning) drugs. Chemotherapy is used to treat conditions of the reticuloendothelial system (lymphomata, leukaemia, etc.), to supplement other forms of treatment for resistant tumours and to treat systemic metastases. These chemotherapeutic agents are classified according to their method of action and/or source.

(1) Alkylating agents   e.g. cyclophosphamide, chlorambucil, thiotepa
(2) Antifolates   e.g. methotrexate
(3) Pyrimidine analogues e.g. 5-fluorouracil
(4) Purine analogues   e.g. mercaptopurine
(5) Plant alkaloids   e.g. vincristine, vinblastine
(6) Miscellaneous group   e.g. (a) platinum compounds; (b) hydroxyurea; (c) hexamethylmelamine.

Most of these drugs are supplied in solid or concentrated form, and are prepared for administration by being dissolved or diluted with the appropriate sterile fluid. The fluid used depends on the drug, and may be water, saline or glucose solution. Once the drugs have been prepared, they are unstable and must be used within a limited time. An adequate supply of sterile fluids must be kept for this purpose.

These drugs affect normal cells as well as the abnormal, particularly those of the blood-producing tissues. The blood count must be closely monitored. The platelet count is likely to be affected. The method of recording drug dosage is usually to show it on a graph with the blood count so that changes in the blood can be observed and even forecast. There is usually a marked systemic effect following administration, characterised by nausea, vomiting and general malaise (feeling unwell). Anti-emetics are given at the same time as the drug as a preventive measure. Other effects include alopecia (loss of hair), stomatitis (soreness of the buccal mucosa) neuritis (nerve pain) and sterility.

In preparing these drugs for administration to the patient, personnel are advised to follow strict safety precautions in order to avoid self-contamination. Gloves and eye-guards should be worn and any spill on the skin should be washed off immediately.

Drugs which increase the effects of radiation

Radiation sensitisers

Certain drugs stimulate cell growth by increasing oxygen uptake. A substance such as Synkavit (vitamin K) may be given with the intention of bringing more cells into the radiation-sensitive phase at the time of irradiation.

Hypoxic cell sensitisers

Oxygen in tissue is a source of electrons when the tissue is irradiated. Cells which lack oxygen have a poor response to radiotherapy (see Chapter 7). This is the case with some tumours (e.g. glioblastoma multiforme). Hypoxic cell sensitisers are substances which have an affinity for electrons. An example is misonidazole, which is given by mouth 4–5 hours prior to irradiation.

CONTRAST MEDIA

A contrast medium is a radio-opaque substance introduced into the body to demonstrate an organ radiographically. Contrast media may be used during treatment planning procedures for localisation purposes:

Hypaque

This is an iodine compound, which is used to demonstrate the renal tract. The compound may be injected into a vein and is rapidly excreted from the blood via the kidneys. It is also introduced into the bladder via a catheter. The procedure is explained in Chapter 6.

Barium sulphate

Barium is a heavy metal and barium sulphate is an inert salt. It is supplied in the form of an emulsion and is used to demonstrate the alimentary tract. In radiotherapy its principal use is as a 'swallow' to demonstrate the oesophagus and oesophageal tumours. Giving a patient a preparation for diagnostic purposes is an 'invasive' procedure and in every case he must be told what is to be done and his consent obtained.

PREPARATIONS FOR EXTERNAL USE

Lotions are preparations for external use. They include skin paint and mild antiseptic solutions for cleaning the skin, and for use as mouth-washes. Other external applications include ointments, creams and dusting powders. These are not subject to drug controls. Disinfectants and strong cleaning agents are stored separately.

METHODS OF ADMINISTRATION

Oral

Many drugs are given by mouth in the form of pills, tablets, capsules and mixtures. In general, pills are sugar-coated to disguise the taste. Tablets and mixtures are quick-acting. Capsules are slow to dissolve and have a long-sustained period of action in the body. Most are swallowed whole but some tablets are prepared in soluble form so that they may be dissolved in water and be easy to swallow. Examples of drugs in solid form are:
(1) analgesics – pain-killing;
(2) anti-emetics – relief of nausea and prevention of sickness;
(3) antibiotics – anti-bacterial;
(4) hormones;
(5) diuretics – acting on the kidneys to increase urine excretion;
(6) anti-diarrhoeal drugs and laxatives.
   The tablets or pills are given to the patient in a small cup, along with a glass of water. The nurse or radiographer must wait while the patient takes them to ensure that he has done so. Mixtures are

poured into a measuring glass, the glass being held at eye level to ensure the correct quantity. If there is a sediment this must be shaken up before the drug is poured. It should be given to the patient, with a glass of water. Examples of drugs in liquid form are: gastric sedatives; anti-diarrhoeals; cough mixture and linctus.

Injection

An injection is an aseptic procedure, but the risk of infection is very low because of the use of disposable needles and syringes. These are supplied in sealed packs sterilised by gamma radiation. Syringes are supplied in a range of sizes from 1 ml to 60 ml. Needles are also available in a range of sizes and are colour-coded:

Orange – fine needles for subcutaneous injections.

Blue – larger needles for intramuscular injections.

Dark green – needles for intravenous injection.

Yellow – large serum needles.

Butterfly needles are a special type of needle for use when a combination of drugs is given intravenously, as is often the case in oncology. They save much discomfort for the patient and excessive damage to the vein. Butterfly needles have small plastic 'wings' attached, which are taped to the skin to prevent movement when it is in the vein, and a plastic tube to which syringes may be fitted in turn.

Drawing-up of drugs

Drugs are supplied in either:

(1)　Glass ampoules which are opened by cutting the end with a small file and breaking it off. The ampoule should always be held in a piece of gauze in case it shatters. The contents are drawn up into the syringe using a large needle or plastic tube.

(2)　A sealed bottle with a rubber cap; here the contents are drawn up by inserting a needle through the cap. The cap must be cleaned with antiseptic solution. The contents of the bottle can only be withdrawn if the air pressure in the bottle is equalised, and to do this a quantity of air is drawn into the syringe through a sterile swab and injected into the bottle as the drug is withdrawn. A fresh needle should be used for the patient.

Rules for drawing-up drugs:

(1)　Read the instructions and follow the correct procedure.

(2)　Ensure that the correct solvent or diluting fluid is used.

(3)   If a combination of drugs is to be prepared, write labels for the syringes beforehand.

(4)   Retain the bottles so that the doctor may see that he is giving the correct drugs.

Injection tray

Equipment

A spirit-soaked Medi-swab to clean the skin at the site of the injection.

Dry cotton-wool swabs to press the area following the injection and prevent bleeding or bruising.

Syringes and needles of the required size.

Drawing-up tubes or needles.

A tourniquet to restrict the blood flow for an intravenous (i.v.) injection.

Small strapping dressings (i.v. injections).

The drug and prescription.

Drugs may be injected intravenously, intramuscularly or subcutaneously.

Subcutaneous injection

A small quantity of the drug is injected under the skin using a fine needle and a small syringe. Examples of subcutaneously injected substances are: local anaesthesia prior to a biopsy of the skin; powerful analgesics such as morphine; tattoo dyes.

Tattooing is used in radiotherapy to delineate the area to be irradiated, and it has certain distinct advantages over other methods of defining the area:

(1)   The marks are very discreet, being only a small black or blue spot (or spots).

(2)   They are permanent and cannot be lost even from parts of the body where skin paint would not remain for long. They allow a greater degree of hygiene because the patient has no anxiety about removal of the marks while washing, and there is no risk of staining the clothing (as is the case with skin paint).

(3)   Should the patient require a further course of treatment at a later date, the previously irradiated areas are easily identifiable. This may be important when a recurrence of the disease is likely and necrosis due to over-irradiation of the tissues must be avoided.

The main disadvantage of tattooing is that some patients dislike the idea very much.

It is usual to mark the field centre and at least two corners or points on the edge of the field which may be aligned with the cross wires of the light beam diaphragm.

Equipment

A Medi-swab to clean the site.
A tattooing or serum needle.
Dye in a dropper bottle – Indian ink, methylene blue or gentian violet.
Sterile dry swabs and sterile moistened swabs.

Procedure

(1)   Clean the skin and wipe it dry.
(2)   Put a small drop of dye on the skin. Make two small punctures into the skin through the dye, going no deeper than the subcutaneous layer.
(3)   Wipe off the surplus dye with a moistened swab (not surgical spirit).
(4)   When tattooing is carried out with a serum needle, two punctures should be made to ensure that the tattoo mark will be distinct from a natural mark.
(5)   A tattooing needle makes three small punctures simultaneously, but unless it is properly sterilised for each patient the risk of infection is high. A disposable needle is safer.

Intramuscular injection

A larger quantity of a drug is introduced into a large muscle where it can be accommodated without undue discomfort until it is absorbed. A larger needle is used than for a subcutaneous injection. The sites for intramuscular injections are the gluteus, quadriceps and deltoid muscles. Great care must be taken to select the correct spot for the injection in order not to damage a nerve and to make sure that the needle is not in a vein by withdrawing the plunger before injecting the drug.

Examples of drugs given intramuscularly are antibiotics and hormones. In both cases slow absorption over a period of time is required to provide a continuous dose. When a course of injections is prescribed, they are spaced to provide continuity.

Intravenous injection
Drugs injected into a vein pass quickly into the circulation and are distributed rapidly around the body. The most common site for the injection in the vein is the antecubital fossa (front of the elbow). A vein in the back of the hand or the forearm may also be used. Unless the veins are small and difficult to enter, a fairly large needle is used.

Procedure
The patient is seated with the arm supported and the blood flow restricted by a tourniquet round the upper arm. This enlarges the vein. The tourniquet is released as soon as the needle has entered the vein and blood can be drawn back into the syringe. When the injection is complete, firm pressure is applied to the site to prevent bleeding and the formation of a haematoma (bruising and blood clot). A small dressing is applied.

Examples of substances given intravenously include:
(1)   those which are required to produce widespread and rapid effect – cytotoxic drugs and radioactive scanning materials;
(2)   large quantities of fluid – blood, intravenous saline, etc.;
(3)   radiographic contrast media – intravenous urography.

Instilled

A drug may be instilled into the eye in the form of drops administered by an eye dropper. This is most easily done if the patient is comfortably positioned on a couch. The upper eyelid is lifted slightly and a drop placed on the upper half of the eye. Care must be taken not to touch the eye with the eye dropper (this is painful) or to drop the fluid from too great a distance. Tears secreted by the lachrymal gland will wash the solution over the surface of the eye. A soft tissue should be provided to remove excess tears and the eye should be dabbed – not rubbed.

Examples of drugs administered in this way are: local anaesthesia prior to inserting an internal lead eyeshield to protect the eye from radiation; bacteriostatic drops to inhibit infection.

Drugs may also be instilled into the pleural and peritoneal cavities when secondary malignant disease has caused a collection of fluid (pleural effusion or abdominal ascites). The fluid is tapped to give the patient relief and a drug such as thiotepa, or *Corynebacterium parvum (C. parvum)* instilled into the cavity to prevent re-collection of the fluid. This is an aseptic procedure.

Applications

These include creams, ointments, lotions, etc., which are applied to the skin or the mucosa. When an application is used a small quantity is transferred from the container to a gallipot (in the case of liquids) or to a piece of sterile gauze (in the case of creams or ointments) and the cover of the container replaced immediately.

Creams and ointments are applied to wounds to assist healing. The wound must be first cleaned to allow the application to reach the surface. Dusting powders may be fungicidal (for foot complaints) or may be used simply to prevent friction in the creases of the body. Patients undergoing radiotherapy are advised to use 'baby' powder liberally on the irradiated skin for this purpose.

Paints are applied with a soft swab or brush. They are used to treat skin infections, inhibit bacterial growth and to delineate the field edges in radiotherapy.

Skin paint

Paint used to mark the treatment area in radiotherapy must have certain properties.
(1) it must be a good indelible stain and difficult to remove;
(2) it must be non-injurious and have a low incidence of allergy – this is important because the skin will be subjected to injury from the radiation;
(3) it must be non-metallic so that the skin reaction around the marks is not increased by scattered electrons from the dye;
(4) it should be easy to obtain – a substance which is expensive or difficult to come by is a nuisance.

The dye in most common use in radiotherapy departments is paint of magenta. Magenta is a crystalline substance which is soluble in alcohol. Once the crystals are dissolved, water may be added to make an aqueous solution. The main advantage of this paint over others is that it does not dissolve in water, and therefore once it has dried on the skin, it is insoluble in the skin moisture and unlikely to smudge or be removed easily.

Application of skin paint

Skin paint is applied with a wooden applicator on which a very small amount of cotton wool has been twisted. The twist of wool must be as small as possible so that the line drawn on the skin is thin and fine. A fresh applicator is used for each patient. The marks should be allowed to dry on the skin rather than be blotted. This allows the dye to sink into the skin. A dusting of talcum powder will help to 'fix' them. If the skin is greasy, it should be cleaned with surgical spirit before the marks are applied.

At the end of the course of treatment the marks must be allowed to wear off naturally. No attempt should be made to remove them because of the risk of damaging the skin.

As a means of field definition, skin paint has certain disadvantages. Skin marks embarrass the patient when they are on a part of the body not hidden by clothing. This may cause the patient to clean them off. They are liable to be lost in the ordinary processes of washing, or if the area has to be cleaned for dressing. In the process of being touched up or replaced, they may wander from their original site and lead to inaccuracy of treatment. The paint stains the clothing and is difficult to remove by washing.

The use of beam directional shells for the treatment of lesions of the head and neck, and of tattooing, overcome many of these problems.

DRUG REACTIONS

Many drugs have side-effects, some of which are an accepted hazard and for which the doctor will be prepared. Occasionally a patient will have an unusual reaction. This is not common but it is an eventuality which must be foreseen, particularly during intravenous injections.

Hypersensitivity, or an increased reaction in the tissues to foreign substances, is called allergy. Mild allergic reactions are very common; for example, many people are sensitive to pollen and suffer from hay fever. Some drugs, particularly antibiotics may cause similar reactions.

A mild reaction takes the form of: a rash on the skin, usually generalised; watering of the eyes; tightness of the chest; nausea and diarrhoea.

The severity of the reactions varies from person to person and will usually disappear once the cause has been removed. In some cases, antihistamine may be prescribed. Histamine is a chemical substance produced in the tissue in response to injury. It causes the heat, swelling and itching associated with insect bites and is the body's attempt to isolate and remove foreign substance. Antihistamine also has side effects which are similar to those produced by alcohol. These include slowed reactions, and patients whose activities require good reactions, such as driving, should be warned of these.

A severe reaction to a drug will make the patient very ill. There may be circulatory collapse and shock (anaphylaxis). This is a possible reaction following the injection of a compound into a vein. This event must be foreseen and precautions taken:

(1) Before an injection is given intravenously, the patient should be asked about any previous adverse reactions.

(2) Intravenous injections are always given very slowly. During the injection the patient is watched closely for signs of unease. These include sweating, pain in the arm of the injection and blotchy appearance of the skin, tightness of the chest or respiratory distress. The injection must be stopped immediately.

(3) Preparation for resuscitation should be on hand. These include a resuscitation drug tray.

The resuscitation drug tray holds a selection of drugs to be used in emergency. These are controlled drugs and when the tray is not likely to be needed it is kept locked in the drug cupboard. It also holds a supply of syringes, needles, sterile swabs and files to open the ampoules.

The drugs on the tray are likely to be selected from the following:

(1) Adrenaline – a substance produced by the adrenal glands. It raises the blood pressure.

(2) Nikethamide – stimulates the heart.

(3) Aminophyllin – stimulates the respiratory system.

(4) Methedrine – stimulates the nervous system.

(5) Piriton – an antihistamine.

(6) Hydrocortisone – another substance produced by the adrenal cortex.

(7) Calcium gluconate – assists the heart action.

(8) Lignocaine – also assists the heart action.

ABBREVIATIONS ON MEDICAL PRESCRIPTIONS

When a doctor writes a prescription he uses abbreviations, some of which indicate how the drug is to be taken. These are intended for the pharmacy, nursing and other staff who have care of the patient. The patient is told in plain language. The radiographer needs to know some of the more common terms:

Stat.	At once
Nocte	At night
p.r.n.	As required
b.d. or b.i.d.	Twice per day
t.d. or t.i.d.	Three times per day
a.c.	Before meals

These are all abbreviated from Latin terms.

Chapter 6
Examinations and
Investigative Procedures

Certain routine procedures are performed in the radiotherapy department at which a radiographer normally assists. These are related to the patient's progress and response to treatment and to the investigation into the nature and extent of a tumour for purposes of planning or treatment.

BLOOD COUNTS

Examination of the blood affords a great deal of information. Disease processes may alter the cells or their proportions in the blood and the chemical composition of the plasma. Patients undergoing radiotherapy or chemotherapy have regular blood counts to assess their tolerance of the treatment. Blood may be obtained by a finger or ear-lobe prick and by venipuncture.

Prick

Equipment

Tray with Medi-swab and cotton wool balls.
Needles.
Glass slides.
Fine glass tube with suction bulb.
    The equipment is supplied by the haematology laboratory who carry out the procedure.

Procedure

The skin is cleaned and a drop of blood obtained. This is drawn up into the tube and expelled on to one or more slides, where it is allowed to dry.

Venipuncture

When a larger quantity of blood is required it is obtained from a vein. The most commonly used site is the antecubital fossa (front of the elbow).

Equipment

Tray containing:
Medi-swab to clean the skin.
A syringe of a size suited to the amount to be taken.
Hypodermic needles – usually large, so that the blood is drawn up quickly and does not clot.
A ligature to restrict the blood flow.
Tubes to receive the blood appropriate to the test.
Cotton wool balls and small dressings.

Procedure

The patient is seated with the arm supported and the elbow straight. The ligature is applied above the elbow to restrict the flow and enlarge the vein. The restriction is maintained until the blood has been drawn up and released before the needle is removed. Firm pressure is applied over the puncture to prevent bleeding and the formation of a haematoma. A small dressing is taped over it.

When the blood is transferred to the tube from the syringe, the needle should be removed to eliminate the risk of clotting in the needle. Some blood tubes contain chemicals to prevent clotting and preserve the shape of the cells. The tube must be gently rocked to mix the chemical and the blood. It must never be shaken, or the cells will be damaged. Needles must be disposed of safely. A correctly completed request form must accompany the blood sample.

INDIRECT LARYNGOSCOPY
(I.D.L.)

The examination is called indirect because the larynx is seen in a mirror. It is performed frequently to assess the response to treatment and the E.N.T. (ear, nose and throat) trolley is kept permanently prepared for use.

Top shelf

(1) *Head mirror.* This is a concave mirror worn by the doctor. It reflects and focuses the light from the bull's eye lamp, placed behind the patient on to the part to be examined.

(2) *Spirit lamp and matches.* The small glass or metal lamp contains methylated spirit. Laryngeal mirrors are warmed in the flame so that: (a) they will not 'steam up' in the patient's breath and obscure the view; (b) a patient is less likely to 'gag' when a warm mirror is placed at the back of the throat than when a cold one is used.

(3) *Laryngeal mirrors.* These are small mirrors mounted on a long handle. They range in size from 10 mm diameter to 28 mm, and the trolley usually carries the full range. Some mirrors are hinged on the handle so that they may be angled in the mouth for a view of inaccessible parts of the mouth and pharynx. These mirrors must be regularly inspected for loss of silvering or for damage. They are sterilised after use.

(4) *Tongue depressors* (tongue spatulae) may be wood or metal. They are used to hold the tongue and other tissues aside to facilitate inspection. Wooden spatulae are disposable and should be broken after use.

(5) *Auroscopes* are cone-shaped instruments used for examining the ear. They are supplied with a light attachment.

(6) *Nasal speculae* resemble sugar tongs and are used to examine the interior of the nostril.

(7) *Sinus forceps* are thin pointed forceps, either straight or angled, which are used to take hold of or extract material from narrow spaces and sinuses.

(8) *Dental napkins.* Small cotton squares with which the tongue is held forward so that the airway at the back of the mouth is visible. These are folded into narrow strips for use and should be kept covered against airborne bacteria.

(9) *Finger cots.* Small rubber finger covers to be worn when feeling inside the mouth.

(10) *Throat swabs* in sterile tubes, for taking samples of material.

Lower shelf

(1) Denture cartons for false teeth.
(2) Paper tissues.
(3) Drinking glass.

(4) Masks – a mask should be worn if:
  (a) the person examining the patient has a cold;
  (b) the patient has an infectious condition.
(5) Receivers and disposal bags.
(6) *The bull's eye lamp* is a bright light with a focusing lens. It is placed behind the patient's left shoulder and adjusted so that the light shines towards the head mirror. It should be switched off when not in use as it quickly overheats.

Procedure

The patient is asked to loosen the clothes at the neck and remove any false teeth. He sits facing the doctor. When the larynx is examined, the tongue is extruded and held by a dental napkin. This opens the airway and enables the larynx to be seen in the mirror placed at the back of the mouth. The patient is asked to say 'E' and the cords can be seen to move. Most patients tolerate the examination well, especially with practice. Being told to relax and breathe through the mouth helps to avoid gagging.

When the patient cannot tolerate the examination, the back of the throat may be sprayed with anaesthetic in an atomiser bottle. In this case he must be warned to avoid eating or drinking for 2 hours, when the anaesthetic will have worn off.

NEUROLOGICAL EXAMINATIONS

Lesions involving the central nervous system (C.N.S.) make themselves apparent by neurological disturbance and impairment of function. The type of disturbance depends on the part of the system involved. A full C.N.S. examination takes a long time. The patient must be undressed so that the limbs may be examined for muscle tone and co-ordination.

Equipment

Patella hammer.
Tuning forks for hearing tests.
Pins and cotton wool for sensory tests.
Test tubes for hot and cold water for temperature discrimination tests.
Ophthalmoscope.

The ophthalmoscope is an instrument for examining the interior of the eye. It contains a light source and a series of lenses by which each plane of the eye may be brought into focus. When in use, the room lights should be dimmed. This causes the eyes to 'accommodate' to reduced light. The pupils expand, giving a better field of vision.

VAGINAL EXAMINATION (P.V.)

Examination per vagina is carried out:
(1)   to examine the organ for disease and response to treatment;
(2)   to assess the extent of tumours in adjacent organs and to palpate for pelvic masses and enlarged lymph nodes.

Unless there is a special reason (post-surgery or pregnancy) the procedure is not aseptic, but sterilised instruments are used. A male doctor requires a female chaperone during the examination. This role is filled by the nurse or radiographer assisting him. An internal gynaecological examination must not be performed on a minor without parental consent.

Equipment

Disposable gloves in several sizes.
K.Y. jelly. This is a water-soluble, colourless and non-toxic lubricant supplied in sterile tubes.
Swabs to wipe the patient.
Cusco specula in various sizes.
Sponge-holder forceps.
Torch or light to illuminate the interior of the vagina.
Sanitary towels.
Disposal bags for used instruments and swabs.

Procedure

The procedure is explained to the patient. She is positioned on a couch, either on her left side or on her back with the knees bent. Privacy must be assured.

Cervical smear

In some cases a sample of the secretions is obtained for diagnosis or hormone level assessment, in which case equipment in addition to that listed above is required:

Cervical spatulae – small wooden paddle-shaped spatulae.

Glass slides and a pencil. Details must always be written on the ground-glass part of the slide in *pencil*. Ink washes off in the fixing solution.

95% Alcohol in a container to fix the slides.

A request form for the laboratory.

RECTAL EXAMINATION (P.R.)

Examinations per rectum are performed for the same reasons as those per vagina, and the procedure is the same.

Equipment

Disposable gloves in various sizes.

K.Y. jelly.

A proctoscope and light.

Swabs to wipe the patient.

Disposal bags for instruments and swabs.

CYTÓLOGY

Cytology means the study of cells. Malignant cells may be found in samples of material obtained from the patient.

Exfoliative cytology

The absence of a capsule of a malignant tumour enables cells to be shed from epithelial surfaces into body cavities and be identified in fluids from these cavities – urine, sputum, pleural and peritoneal fluids and cerebrospinal fluid.

Specimens of sputum and urine are obtained in the same way as for bacteriological examination and several samples may have to be taken over several days because the cells are few in number.

Specimens of other fluids are aspirated – drawn off in a syringe. Aspiration of fluid from the chest, abdomen or spinal canal is a strictly aseptic procedure and not usually performed in the department. The basic equipment required is:

Antiseptic solution to clean the skin.

Local anaesthesia.

Small syringe and subcutaneous needles for the anaesthetic.

Large syringe for the aspiration.
Cannula or large needle for the aspiration syringe.
Sterile bottle to receive the fluid.
Dressings.
Resuscitation tray in case of shock.

Needle aspiration

A small amount of tissue may be extracted from a tumour mass or
lymph node. The needle used is a lare cannula with a cutting edge so
that a core of tissue is removed.

Equipment

Antiseptic solution and swabs to clean the skin.
Local anaesthesia.
Small syringe and needles for the anaesthetic.
Large syringe (5 ml) for the aspiration.
Cannula.
Bottle of sterile water.
Specimen bottle.
Dressings and resuscitation tray.

Procedure

A small amount of water is drawn up into the aspiration syringe
before the material is extracted from the tumour mass. By expelling
the water, the core of tissue is washed out of the cannula into the
specimen bottle.

Cytological 'scrape'

Cells may be removed from a small surface tumour by scraping. The
material is spread on to glass slides, fixed and dried. It is a method
often used for diagnosis of skin tumours such as basal cell carcinoma.

Equipment

Antiseptic solution and swabs to clean the skin.
Glass slides and fixative in slide container.
Pencil.

Small scalpel blade and Bard-Parker handle.
Gauze dressing and tape.
Cardboard envelopes for prepared slides.
Laboratory request form.

Procedure

After cleaning the area, the lesion is scraped with the scalpel blade
sufficiently to draw blood. The scraping must be done at the edge of
the lesion as this is the actively growing part. Malignant tissue often
has a 'gritty' feeling. The material is spread onto the slides and
placed immediately in the fixative where the slides are left for 20
min, after which they are removed and allowed to dry away from
heat. The area of the scrape is dressed, gentle pressure being used to
stop the bleeding. The procedure is not as cruel as it sounds as many
skin lesions bleed very easily.

EXCISION BIOPSY

A small piece of tissue excised from the tumour yields a great deal of
information about the histology or cell structure. A biopsy is an
aseptic procedure, so a sterile trolley is prepared for the equipment.

Equipment

Antiseptic solution and swabs to clean the skin.
Dressing towels to protect the clean area and give the doctor a sterile
field in which to work.
Local anaesthesia such as 1% amethocaine.
Small syringe and a fine needle to administer it.
A larger needle for drawing up.
No. 11 scalpel blade and Bard-Parker handle.
One pair of rat-toothed forceps to grip the piece of tissue.
Three pairs of plain forceps with which to handle the instruments.
Stitch with fine needle.
Needle-holder or Spencer Wells forceps.
Scissors.
Dressings.
Collodion or nebecutane.
Specimen jar containing formalin.

Morbid anatomy request form.
Resuscitation tray.

Procedure

The area is cleaned and anaesthetised. The anaesthetic must be checked before being given because it comes under the D.D.A. regulations. A small piece of tissue is cut from the edge of the lesion and a stitch inserted to stop the bleeding and close the wound. The wound is dressed with collodion or nubecutane. These are gum-like dressings which form a 'skin' and close the wound. They are preferable to zinc oxide strapping, especially when there is a likelihood of radiotherapy being given. Zinc oxide in the skin increases the skin reaction. Strapping dressings are also very uncomfortable in some situations and painful to remove.

All evidence of blood, etc., should be removed or covered before the patient gets off the couch. After the procedure he may be offered a cup of tea before being allowed to leave. He will return about 1 week later to have the stitch removed, and by that time the pathological report will be available.

TONGUE BIOPSY

A biopsy of a tongue lesion is sometimes done in out-patients clinic, especially if the patient has come from some distance and there is a delay in admitting him. It is an uncomfortable procedure for the patient at the time but the tissues of the mouth heal rapidly.

Equipment

Anaesthetic lozenges (Decicaine).
A receiver.
A biopsy punch.
Gauze swabs.
Dental napkins.
Glyco-thymol mouth-wash.
Ice cubes (depending on the opinion of the medical officer).
Specimen jar with formalin.
Morbid anatomy request form.

Procedure

The patient is given an anaesthetic lozenge to suck and a receiver into which to spit the saliva. He should be told not to swallow it. After about 15 min the mouth will be anaesthetised. The tongue is held by a dental napkin and a small piece of tissue removed with the biopsy punch. Bleeding, which will be copious, is controlled by pressure with sterile gauze held firmly on the wound. Once the bleeding has stopped, glyco-thymol mouth-washes are given and the patient offered ice cubes to suck, as these will also inhibit bleeding. No food or drink should be taken until the anaesthesia has worn off – 1–2 hours. Hot or spicy food should be avoided until the wound heals and aspirin mucilage or soluble aspirin mouth-washes prescribed before meals as required.

Biopsy of deeper structures is a surgical procedure for which a general anaesthetic is required and the patient is admitted to the ward.

PLANNING CYSTOGRAM

A planning cystogram is required when a tumour of the bladder is to be treated. Unlike a diagnostic cystogram, when the intention is to distend the bladder to demonstrate irregularities of the walls, a planning cystogram is intended to localise the position of the bladder accurately in the pelvis. Only a small amount of dye is introduced in order to limit the bladder volume. A small amount of air is introduced with it in order to give a fluid level and a positive contrast which is easily seen on the film.

During the treatment of a bladder tumour it is important to maintain an accurate small volume in the zone of high dosage. In order to achieve this, the patient must be told to empty the bladder before entering the treatment room.

Equipment

This is an aseptic procedure. A cystogram pack is usually supplied by the C.S.S.D. It contains:

Gallipot – to hold antiseptic lotion.
Swabs and gauze and sterile gloves.
Two dressing towels.
Two pairs of plain forceps.

Kidney dish.
Spigot.

Also required:

Foley's or balloon catheters – various sizes.
Skin cleaning fluid.
Anaesthetic lubricant (male patient).
20 ml bladder syringe or 20 ml syringe with catheter attachment.
10 ml syringe.
10 ml sterile water to inflate the balloon.
20 ml Hypaque 45 per cent.
File to open the ampoules.
Drawing-up tube.
Tape and scissors.
Resuscitation tray in case of shock.
Rectal examination tray – the doctor may wish to ascertain the extent
  of the tumour via the rectum and to feel for pelvic nodes.

Procedure

The patient is catheterised by the doctor or nurse; 10 ml of water is
injected into the balloon of the catheter to keep it in place. The water
must be sterile in case the balloon bursts. 20 ml of dye is introduced
into the bladder along with 5 ml of air. Planning films must then be
taken with minimal delay because urine entering the bladder dilutes
the dye and adds to the quantity of fluid.

Unlike a diagnostic procedure, it is not usually thought necessary
to prepare the patient by restricting fluids for a planning cystogram.

TUMOURS OF THE PROSTATE

The planning procedure is the same but the dye is introduced into
the balloon of the catheter and not into the bladder. This enables the
neck of the bladder to be localised.

PLANNING INTRAVENOUS UROGRAPHY
(I.V.U.)

An intravenous urogram is performed to localise the position of the
kidneys, usually to shield them during the treatment of abdominal
lymph nodes (lower mantle technique).

Unlike the diagnostic procedure, the patient does not usually have to be prepared beforehand by restricting fluids, and therefore the detail obtained is not as good as that obtained by the X-ray department. It is an aseptic procedure.

The injection of an iodine dye always carries a risk of anaphylactic shock and this event must be foreseen.

Equipment

Medi-swabs.
Cotton-wool balls.
10 ml syringe.
Intravenous needles and drawing-up needles.
10 ml Hypaque 45 per cent.
File to open to ampoule.
Tourniquet to restrict the blood flow.
Dressings.
Resuscitation tray.

Procedure

The dye is injected into a vein in the antecubital fossa. The patient usually experiences slight tingling in the arm and saltiness in the mouth during the injection, but if there is any tightness of the chest or pain, the injection must be discontinued. The dye begins to concentrate in normal kidneys from about 5 min after the injection.

BARIUM SWALLOW

A barium swallow is required for planning tumours of the oesophagus. The purpose is to demonstrate the position of the tumour in the oesophagus by narrowing or obstruction. A swallow may also be required to demonstrate displacement of the oesophagus.

In general, only a small quantity of barium is used and, because patients with tumours of the oesophagus have difficulty in swallowing, the barium is fairly thin. A vomit bowl and a glass of water must always be available during the procedure.

The barium is supplied in sealed cans, like soft drink cans, and the can should be shaken before opening to mix the sediment. The barium is poured into a drinking cup and a flexible straw provided.

The straw is necessary because most patients are positioned on the couch and cannot sit up to drink.

The passage of the barium may be seen during fluoroscopy. When a film is to be taken the patient is told to take a mouthful of barium and hold it until told to swallow just before the exposure is made. He must be given time to swallow and remain still before the film is taken. After the procedure, the patient should be offered a glass of water and tissues to wipe the mouth. Open cans of barium should be discarded.

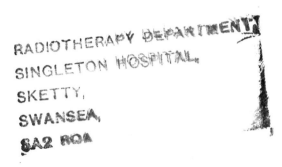

Chapter 7
The Effects of
Radiation on Tissue

Ionising radiation causes damage to living cells. There is no essential difference between its effect on normal cells and abnormal cells. The damage is brought about by electrons liberated in the tissues when radiation is absorbed. The degree of damage depends on:
(1)   the mitotic rate of the cell and to some extent its state at the time of irradiation;
(2)   the radiation dosage;
(3)   the amount of oxygen in the tissues.

MITOSIS AND THE MITOTIC RATE
OF THE CELL

A cell consists of three parts:
(1)   The nucleus – the life centre of the cell in which the processes of reproduction take place.
(2)   The cytoplasm – the body of the cell. Chemical processes in the cytoplasm make use of the food and oxygen absorbed from the blood for the cell's survival and for the manufacture of cell secretions.
(3)   The cell membrane – the membrane encloses the cell and protects it. It permits the entry of food and oxygen and the excretion of waste and cell secretions.

The nucleus contains chromatic granules which form chromosomes. The word chromosomes is made up of two Greek words: *chroma*, colour and *soma*, body. When the cell is stained for microscopy, the chromosomes take up the dye. The chromosomes carry genes which determine the characteristics of the cell and the organism to which it belongs.

Cells reproduce by a process of division called mitosis. In the process of mitosis, the cell passes through several stages:
(1)   the chromosomes become organised into a coil;
(2)   they divide into an equal number of segments, splitting longitudinally;

89

(3) these travel to opposite ends of the cell;
(4) the chromosomes take up their former appearance;
(5) the cytoplasm divides, forming two identical 'daughter' cells;
(6) The cell has a resting phase.

The various appearances of the cell during this process are called mitotic figures. The most vulnerable phase in this process for a cell exposed to radiation is (2), when it is actively preparing to divide. The least vulnerable is (6).

Tissues which undergo many mitoses in a short time grow quickly – the skin, bone marrow, reproductive cells and juvenile organisms, and because many of their cells are active at any one time, tumours arising in these tissues are radiosensitive.

Tissues which grow slowly – bone, cartilage, fibrous and nervous tissue – are radioresistant. Tumours arising on these tissues are also radioresistant.

The degree of differentiation of a tumour cell affects its sensitivity to radiation. Normal cells are distinct in appearance and can be recognised as belonging to a particular type of tissue. They are well differentiated. Cells which have undergone malignant change lose their distinctive appearance and show various degrees of differentiation from moderately well differentiated to undifferentiated (anaplastic). Poorly differentiated tumours usually grow quickly and have a rapid response to radiation, but this does not necessarily make them radiocurable. They tend to disseminate early and are often generalised when the patient presents for treatment. This limits what may be safely done with radiotherapy. A tumour that is moderately well differentiated has the best chance of being radiocurable.

RESPONSE TO RADIATION

Immediately following a dose of radiation, there is a latent period of from 6 to 24 hours. After this several things may take place:
(1) immediate cell death due to damage to the nucleus;
(2) delayed death due to damage to the cytoplasm or the membrane;
(3) apparent recovery, but the cell will age prematurely;
(4) damage to the chromosomes resulting in the production of abnormal daughter cells. Some of these will die through inability to divide.

In general, large doses of radiation result in (1) and (2), while small doses result in (3) and (4).

RADIATION DOSAGE

A dose of radiation prescribed for the treatment of a tumour is divided into fractions, and the patient is treated at prescribed intervals, the most common being three or five times per week. The biological effect of the radiation is partly dependent on the fractionation intervals. This is a complicated subject, but depending on the dose at each treatment and the number of treatments per week, radiobiologically equivalent doses may be calculated using Ellis's Tables (published dosage data). When a dose of radiation is given in fractions, a larger total dose must be given to produce the same effect as would have taken place had it all been given at one session. For example: 2000 cGy given at one session will have an effect similar to that produced by a total dose of 4200 cGy given in even daily fractions over 28 days. In practice, except for very small lesions and in certain situations, such large doses are not given in one session. The effect of radiation on the tumour is increased by fractionation. Some of the reasons for this are: ongoing mitoses result in a fresh group of cells being in the sensitive phase at different times and therefore more likely to be destroyed. In some cases fractionation appears to make the tumour more sensitive, possibly due to an increase in the blood supply in the surrounding tissues as a result of the radiation reaction. Changes may also take place in the tumour itself as a result of alteration of its sensitivity following irradiation. The changes in sensitivity may be due to changes in the mitotic pattern in the tumour and to cell damage.

The induction of partial synchrony (more cells reach the same phase simultaneously) in the surviving cells of the tumour and radiation damage to cells in the tissues around it may also help in its destruction.

It is important that, when a course of radiotherapy is begun, there is not a long interval between the first and second doses. Once the course is started it should continue unbroken. In many cases a second dose of radiation given 24 hours after the first has a slightly greater effect, possibly due to the latent period.

In the treatment of non-malignant conditions the fractionation interval is not so important. Very few non-malignant conditions are irradiated nowadays because the dangers of ionising radiation have been recognised, but there are a few which benefit from this form of treatment.

THE EFFECT OF OXYGEN

Vascular tissue (tissue well supplied with blood vessels) is more sensitive to radiation than tissue which is poorly supplied (avascular).

The reason for this increased sensitivity is due to the blood carrying oxygen to the tissues. Radiation is effective in tissue because when it is absorbed it is converted into electrons. Oxygen (O_{16}^8) is a source of electrons. Actively growing tissue has a good blood supply. Slow-growing tissue is less well supplied. A malignant tumour is usually well supplied with blood because the blood vessels in the tissues around it enlarge to fulfil the tumour's demand, often to the detriment of these tissues. The tumour may therefore be more sensitive to treatment than the normal tissues in which it is growing. However, as the tumour becomes larger, it may outstrip its blood supply and part of it will die and form a bloodless hypoxic core. This will be resistant to radiation and this is very often the cause of failure to destroy the tumour by irradiation alone.

Benign tumours have a poor blood supply, usually because they are dependent on the supply entering the stalk of the capsule which encloses them. The capsule itself forms an anoxic (oxygen-free) barrier between the tumour and electrons generated in the surrounding tissues.

Certain factors diminish the amount of oxygen in the tissues
(1) The presence of sepsis or necrotic tissue in the irradiated zone. For this reason, tumour residue may be removed by surgery, particularly when irradiation has made a previously inoperable tumour operable.
(2) Scar tissue resulting from surgery or previous irradiation.
(3) Anaemia. A deficiency of haemoglobin or red cells in the blood affects the capacity of the blood to carry oxygen to the tissues.

METHODS OF INCREASING THE SENSITIVITY OF THE TISSUES TO RADIATION

(1) The first and most important step is to determine the level of haemoglobin (Hb) and correct anaemia prior to starting treatment. The normal values of Hb are:
    13.5–16 mg per 100 ml of blood in men;
    11.0–16 mg per 100 ml of blood in women;
The lowest acceptable value in patients to be treated by radiation is:
    10 mg per 100 ml (or 70 per cent in old terminology).
In severe anaemia, the most effective way of raising the Hb is by blood transfusion.
(2) Drugs may be used to increase the effect of radiation (see Chapter 5).

(3) Artificially increasing the oxygen tension in the tissues by causing the patient to breathe pure oxygen while being treated. This is done by placing the patient in a pressurised oxygen-filled tank (hyperbaric tank). When oxygen is breathed under pressure, the haemoglobin is 100 per cent saturated, and excess oxygen is dissolved in the plasma from where it reaches the tissues by diffusion from the capillaries. This method is very effective, but the technique has certain limitations.

Indications for hyperbaric oxygen

(1)   Radiotherapy. Irradiation of hypoxic tumours.
(2)   The treatment of Clostridial gas gangrene. *Clostridium welchii* is a true anaerobe, and saturation of the tissues with oxygen prevents the growth of the organisms.
(3)   The treatment of intractable surface infections – burns, bedsores, varicose ulcers and ischaemic (bloodless) grafts.

Hyperbaric oxygen in radiotherapy

Technique

The treatment is given via a glass or Perspex viewing window in a sealed stainless-steel tank. The patient is positioned in the tank prior to pressurisation. This limits the treatment techniques to simple field arrangements. Another limiting factor is the time to bring the tank up to pressure and carry out the treatment. This is from ½ to 1 hour. Pressurisation takes about 15 minutes. A pressure of 45 lbs/in^2 is equal to three atmospheres – two above normal.

At higher pressures convulsions are more likely to occur. At lower pressures the plasma is not saturated. The pressure is maintained for 10–15 minutes to allow saturation of the plasma before treatment is given. Some centres monitor the pulse and respiration during the saturation period, but others consider the electrical risk too great. After treatment, decompression is carried out fairly quickly and the oxygen piped out of the department and not released in the room.

Dosage

The sensitivity of the tissues is greatly increased and the dosages are lower than for conventional radiotherapy. On average a dose level of two-thirds of that required in conventional treatment is used. The normal tissue reactions are more marked. In most cases the patients are treated two or three times per week. This is partly because of the technicalities involved and patient tolerance, but it has also been shown that, when treating with hyperbaric oxygen, the results of few large doses given twice per week are superior to smaller doses given daily.

Patient care and preparation

The preparation of the patient for hyperbaric treatment is very important. Many refuse because of claustrophobia; some have to be anaesthetised. Most patients require a mild sedative before being treated.

Raised atmospheric pressure causes pain in the ears. This may be relieved by yawning or swallowing or by sucking sweets. The patient is given a lollipop to suck in the tank, but in some cases myringotomy is performed (see below). Conditions which affect the ears and the Eustachian tubes – for instance the common cold – are contraindications for treatment.

Dentures and all jewellery are removed prior to treatment. This is in case of convulsions and the risk of injury. In some cases water and a vomit bowl are supplied in the tank. The interior of the tank becomes very warm and the patient wears only a cotton gown and cotton socks. All the other linen in the tank is made of cotton. No man-made fibre is used because of the risk of static electricity and sparking.

Hazards

Fire

Materials which are inflammable are 1000 times more so in oxygen than in air. 'Flash' burns will ignite the skin, clothing and hair. For this reason all efforts are made to eliminate any sparking from electrical equipment or from static. Electrical sources include connections to monitoring equipment, bells and switches which may be connected to the tank. It also includes the treatment unit itself. Many centres favour a cobalt 60 unit rather than a linear accelerator for use with an oxygen tank for this reason. This is also the reason for the oxygen being pumped out of the department after use and not released into the treatment room. Static electricity is eliminated by the use of natural fibres for all linen used in the tank. The equipment in the treatment room must also be anti-static.

Oxygen toxicity

Pure oxygen breathed for a period of time is toxic to the cells, and the patient must be carefully watched during the period of pressurisation for signs of toxicity. These include: a feeling of unease; sweating and palpitations; twitching and convulsions. If these signs occur the patient must be returned to breathing air as quickly as possible, and decompression carried out rapidly.

Otitic barotrauma

If the Eustachian tubes cannot be cleared by yawning or swallowing, or if the tubes are blocked, damage to the tympanic membranes may occur. Oxygen is absorbed from the middle ear more rapidly than air and aural atelectasis – collapse of the membrane – may take place. This causes pain and deafness. Meringotomy may be performed before treatment is undertaken, to prevent this. This involves the insertion of a small hollow tube into the tympanic membrane which does not affect the hearing and will allow for pressure adjustment.

Pulmonary atelectasis

A blocked air passage in the lung may cause the part of the lung beyond the block to collapse through oxygen being absorbed from it and not being replaced from outside. Chest infections with sputum and mucus, which may block an air passage, are contraindications for treatment in a hyperbaric tank.

General hygiene

Strict hygiene is important in the tank where warmth, moisture from the patient and the presence of oxygen all contribute to an incubation site for bacteria.

Late effects of radiation

(1) Cells which have been damaged or aged by radiation do not easily tolerate further injury. Such injury includes more radiation,

surgery, pressure and friction, exposure to strong sunlight and other forms of heat. Tissues are very rarely irradiated to the limits of their tolerance. To do so is to risk causing necrosis (death of tissues) at a later date.

(2)   Cells in which the chromosomes have been damaged as a result of small doses may continue to divide and produce abnormal daughter cells. Some of the abnormalities seen in these cells are identical to those observed in malignant cells. Radiation-induced malignancy takes many years to become apparent in the patient. This is because of the time-scale required for a few cells to multiply into the many millions which make up a visible tumour. The usual period is from 25 to 30 years.

Chapter 8
Radiation Reactions
and Care of the Patient

THE SYSTEMIC REACTION

A dose of radiation produces a systemic reaction in the patient. This usually appears 6–12 hours after the radiation has been given. In some cases when a very large dose has been given, or when a very large volume of tissue has been irradiated, it may appear sooner. This is one of the problems in whole-body treatment – the time taken to deliver the dose is long and the patient may begin to feel ill before completion of delivery.

The systemic reaction varies in severity and the degree of severity depends on several factors. These will be discussed below. The symptoms of the systemic reaction include:
(1) tiredness and lassitude;
(2) depression;
(3) anorexia (loss of appetite);
(4) nausea;
(5) vomiting – in severe radiation exposure, the vomiting may be uncontrolled, leading to collapse from dehydration and exhaustion.

The effects will be intensified by local mucosal reactions which will contribute to fluid loss from the body (for example, diarrhoea). The mucosal reactions and a drop in the white blood cell count will place the patient at risk by making him infection prone. Extreme reactions should never occur as a result of radiation treatment.

CAUSES OF THE REACTION

Toxicity from the breakdown products of protein

Cells which are damaged or are killed as a result of the radiation are removed and broken down by phagocytic action. The breakdown products enter the blood stream and are eliminated via the kidneys. The presence of toxic products in the blood makes the patient feel unwell and produce, in particular symptoms (1), (2) and (3). The latent period of 6–12 hours is the same as that required for cell damage to become apparent following irradiation.

The response of the tissues to the radiation affects the severity of the reaction

This is a very important factor in the treatment of certain lesions and certain parts of the body. Some tissues are very much more sensitive than others. When a large volume of sensitive tissue is irradiated – for instance the spinal column and the ribs which contain bone marrow – a marked systemic reaction may be expected.

Secondly, certain tumours respond much more readily to treatment than others. The rapid breakdown and absorption of a sensitive tumour such as a lymphosarcoma could make the patient feel very ill indeed.

Alteration in the body chemistry

It is possible that the destruction of a large number of cells and the effects of radiation on the body produce changes in the body chemistry which make the patient feel unwell.

The effect of radiation on the white cell count

This is also contributory, and is discussed in the following section.

Psychogenic

In many cases, if a person believes he is going to feel ill he will do so. Radiotherapy has a certain mystery for most people, and it seems natural that they should experience a reaction after treatment. The systemic reaction is certainly not all 'in the mind', but to tell a patient he is going to feel ill will usually ensure that he does so. This often presents difficulty in the radiotherapy department because patients in the waiting room exchange gossip and symptoms. The best that can be done is to explain to the patient what he is to expect, encourage him to report any reactions and tell him not to believe all he hears from other patients.

REDUCING THE SYSTEMIC REACTION

A basic principle in medicine is not to hurt the patient. Tolerance of the treatment is of great importance. The general policy in radiotherapy is to treat the tumour as quickly as possible, but if the treatment makes the patient feel too ill, he may refuse to come back for more! Methods of reducing the systemic reaction to radiation include:

Fractionation of dosage

A large total dose of radiation is tolerated without difficulty if it is divided into small fractions and given over several weeks. The size of the fractions depends on the volume of tissue to be irradiated – the larger the volume, the smaller the fraction. If the volume is very large, treatment may be begun slowly, increasing to full dosage over a few days as the patient's tolerance is assessed. As a general rule, tumours in the body receive 1000 cGy per week. Treatment is usually given five times per week – Monday to Friday with two days off at the weekend. This is as much a matter of convenience for the patient as well as for the staff. The course of treatment is tiring and reactions build up towards the end of the week. The patient needs a short rest at regular intervals.

The beam energy

A great advantage of megavoltage radiation is that the systemic reactions are not as great as with orthovoltage. This is because of the lower absorption of radiation in the tissues. This is of particular importance when the patient is very fat and the total volume irradiated will consequently be very large.

The care of the patient

(1) At the commencement of treatment the patient should be told not to expect any major reaction to the treatment. He may be told that he can expect to feel tired, and be advised to rest as and when he feels the need. He should not be told that he will feel sick or ill. The radiographer should make enquiries regarding his general health and try to assess his condition before each treatment. If the patient states that he has been sick, it is important to find out whether he has

actually vomited and, if so, how often and how soon after treatment. Symptoms of nausea are usually most noticeable at the beginning of the course and tend to become less as the patient comes to tolerate the dosage. Nausea due to radiation reaction does not occur for the first time in the middle or towards the end of a course.

In this case, or if the nausea persists, the medical officer must be informed. It could be due to another disease process – for instance, a rise in the blood calcium due to bone metastases. Hormone therapy also sometimes causes nausea.

(2)   Fluid intake: increased fluids help to eliminate toxic products from the blood. It is difficult to advise a patient on just how much to drink, as needs vary from one person to another. However a large glass of water with each meal, and an extra cup of tea or coffee, will add about 2 pints to the daily intake.

(3)   Diet: the diet of a patient undergoing radiotherapy should be light and nourishing. In many respects, a patient who is at home with someone to give him a little of what he likes in the way of meals does better than a patient on the ward. Meal-times can be more flexible. The patient may find small meals at more frequent intervals easier to manage than larger meals at the regular times.

Sometimes the patient will take a dislike to certain foods or drinks or complain of a nasty taste in the mouth even when the mouth is not included in the field of radiation. Attention to mouth hygiene and sharp-tasting and fizzy drinks often help this, and relieve nausea. Extra vitamins also help to promote the patient's feeling of well-being and create an appetite. Vitamin C in particular helps to heal the mucosa. In some cases, green vegetables and fruit in the diet are restricted, but a daily supply of citrus fruit juice or tomato juice should replace the deficiency.

Appetite stimulants

Whenever possible, the patient should be encouraged to get up, get dressed and go out. Being up and about increases the feeling of well-being and normality. Fresh air increases the metabolism and consequently the appetite. Alcohol in small quantities stimulates the appetite. If the patient likes a glass of sherry or wine and there is no medical reason to withhold it, he should have it. Similarly, with beer or Guinness, which is usually offered to patients in radiotherapy wards at lunch-time. Guinness is nourishing in itself because it contains sugar and vitamin B.

Specific remedies

When a patient is troubled by nausea and lacks appetite, anti-emetic and appetite-stimulating preparations may be prescribed. Pyridoxine (vitamin B) has been used for a long time in radiotherapy. Its disadvantage is that it is expensive. Other drugs in use are Torecan, 10 mg b.d., and Stematil, 5 mg b.d. These drugs are usually given by mouth but if the patient is actually vomiting, anti-emetics may be given by injection. If the patient is a diabetic, his diet requires careful attention and the co-operation of the diabetic clinic should be sought. Loss of appetite and nausea, together with local reactions on the mucosa, may cause changes in the blood sugar. Adjustments may be necessary to insulin dosage. Attention should also be paid to the necessity for regular meal-times.

THE BLOOD

The effect of radiation on the blood probably contributes to the systemic reaction in the patient. Radiation causes a drop in the white cell count (leucopenia). The severity of the effect depends on the volume of haemopoietic tissue included in the field – bone marrow, and lymphatic tissue – and the volume of the circulating blood irradiated.

Irradiation of the blood-forming organs depresses the production of new cells. The reduction in numbers is seen first in the white cells, the lymphocytes being the most sensitive. Changes in the red cell count and haemoglobin as a result of radiation are not apparent during and immediately following a course of treatment. This is because the red cells have a long life (120 days) and are practically unaffected by radiation. There is not usually an immediate change in the platelet count, but it starts to fall later.

CARE OF THE PATIENT

Prior to starting a course of radiation therapy, a full blood count and differential is obtained. The differential is a statement of the percentages of the various groups of cells. This blood count forms a 'base line' from which changes brought about by the radiation may be monitored.

The normal values of the white cell count are:

Total count: 5000–10,000 per ml of blood

Lymphoid cells: lymphocytes, 20%
                  monocytes, 5%
Myeloid cells: neutrophils, 70%
                  eosinophils, 4%
                  basophils, 1%

The count is repeated at regular intervals during the course. In most cases weekly counts are sufficient, but when large volumes of tissue are irradiated or when a large amount of blood-forming tissue is included in the field, repeat blood counts are done more frequently.

In recording and monitoring the blood count it is important to note the rate at which the white count falls. Most patients show a slow decline in the number of white cells over the period of the treatment. At the end of the course the total white cell count is still at a tolerable level. If however the count shows a marked drop in the first 1–2 weeks of treatment, care must be exercised and the medical officer's attention drawn to it. It is possible that some other cause is contributing to the drop in the white cell count. The patient may have very little functioning bone marrow, for example, or have been given a cytotoxic drug prior to starting the course.

In cases where the white cell count shows a rapid drop it is usual to record the count on a graph so that the probable rate of decline may be forecast (see Figure 2). A total white count of 3000 per ml of blood is generally accepted as the lowest 'safe' level at which treatment may be given. Below this level, radiation should not be given without consultation with the medical officer. It must be remembered that, once the course of radiation treatment has finished, the white cell count will continue to fall for a week or two before recovering and returning to normal. This is probably a contributing factor to the patient feeling tired and rather ill by the end of the course, and for about a week after it. The time taken by the count to recover is about 4 weeks.

Other factors affecting the blood count

Chemotherapy

Many of the drugs used in chemotherapy have a marked effect on the blood count in much the same way as radiation. They are taken up selectively by active cells, i.e. those of the bone marrow. Cells which are radiosensitive are also drug-sensitive. Chemotherapy often

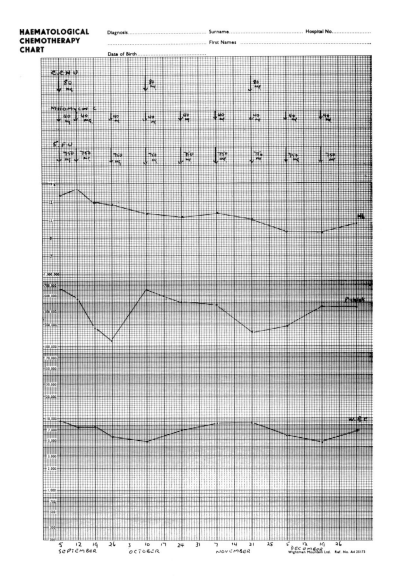

Figure 2. Blood count graph. (By permission of the Radiotherapy Department, Royal Free Hospital, London).

affects the platelet count as well as the white cell count. The platelet count is usually included in a routine blood test as a matter of course.

In some cases chemotherapy supplements radiation, and the blood count must be very carefully monitored.

The normal platelet count is 250,000–400,000 per ml of blood. a platelet count of under 100,000 per ml is dangerous. At this level there is a risk of bleeding from the mucosa and from the capillary vessels under the skin. Sub-epithelial bleeding shows as small red spots, usually seen first on the fronts of the legs and palate. These are called petechiae. This situation is not common.

Disease affecting the bone marrow and blood-forming organs

The production of blood cells may be depressed in widespread metastatic disease with bone involvement. Leukaemia also causes marked changes in the blood count.

Infections

A bacterial infection raises the white cell count due to the increased production of myeloid cells. A virus infection causes a drop in the count, due to the destruction of the cells by the virus.

Toxic erythema

This is a very rare but dangerous reaction to radiation. It is characterised by a skin rash and complete aplasia (no cell formation) of the blood-forming organs. The patient feels very ill. Eruptions on the skin are common and the radiographer must be sufficiently observant to look at the skin outside the irradiated area and note any abnormal signs. This is particularly important during the first part of the course. The most likely cause of a skin rash is an antibiotic.

Late changes in the blood

Large doses of radiation to the blood-forming organs cause permanent cessation of cell formation. When only part of the body is treated, blood-forming tissue elsewhere in the body compensates.

When many areas of the body are irradiated – for example, for many bone metastases, the blood count will eventually show abnormal proportions. This is because the production of cells by the bone marrow is suppressed or diminished and the lymphatic tissue compensates. There will also be a reduction in the red cell count.

Whole-body irradiation (depending on the dose) brings about a marked drop in cell formation and even complete aplasia. The 50% lethal dose is 400 cGy in 30 days (LD50/30 = 400 cGy).

Exposure to small doses of radiation over a period of time may cause changes in the bone marrow which give rise to the production of abnormal cells. Radiation-induced leukaemia is a hazard of working with radiation without proper protection.

Methods of reducing the effects on the blood

(1)   The use of megavoltage radiation spares the bone marrow because of the low differential absorption in bone.
(2)   Planning to avoid blood-producing tissue and shielding bone when it is not necessary to include it in the field.
(3)   The avoidance of virus infections by hygiene in the department, and by advice given to the patient.

THE SKIN, AND CARE OF SKIN REACTIONS

The skin is the part of the body which is always included in the field because it cannot be avoided. Every effort must be made therefore to reduce the effects of radiation on it, and to avoid damage as far as is possible.

The skin is an important tissue for the efficient functioning of the body. Its functions include:
(1)   protection of the tissues;
(2)   heat control of the body;
(3)   excretion of waste;
(4)   sensory information;
(5)   vitamin D production.

It is composed of various layers, each of which may be affected by radiation, depending on the beam energy. These layers are:
(1)   Subcutaneous layer – an elastic layer composed of fatty fibrous tissue. It contains blood vessels and lymphatics, nerve endings, hair follicles, sweat and sebaceous glands.
(2)   Germinal layer – composed of columnar cells in constant division, replacing cells lost from the skin surface. It is often called the basal layer.

(3)   Epidermis – made up of layers of cells: prickle cells, clear cells, keratinous or horny cells.

The average skin thickness is 3 mm. The vitality of the skin is affected by the general health of the subject. A debilitating illness, loss of mobility and poor nourishment devitalise the skin and make it more easily injured. If a patient is bed-ridden, pressure sores may develop on areas subjected to pressure – the sacral area, the heels especially – unless steps are taken to prevent it. Once pressure sores have formed they may be difficult to heal and can easily become infected. Devitalised skin has a poor tolerance of injury, including radiation.

The skin is the site of several tumours which are treated by irradiation. In many cases, radiotherapy is the treatment of choice because, if carried out with care, the scarring is minimal and the cosmetic effect excellent. This is especially important for lesions on the face and it is lack of care in these situations which gives radiotherapy a bad name.

THE ACUTE REACTION

The classic signs of injury are: heat, redness, swelling, discomfort, and loss of function. These signs are produced on the skin by radiation. The degree of severity of the reactions depends on the dose of radiation given – total dosage and fractionation intervals – and on the beam quality and other factors which will be discussed below.

Skin reactions are divided into stages (see Figure 3):

The first 24 hours

In the first 24 hours following a dose of radiation, a transient 'warmth' is usually noticed at the site of the treatment. Further irradiation produces an erythema or reddening of the skin.

First-degree erythema

The skin is slightly reddened or mottled. At low energy this appears at a dose level of 1000–2000 cGy. At megavoltage a higher dose is required. If no further treatment is given, it fades to a pale tan.

Second-degree erythema

If treatment is continued on the first-degree reaction, the skin will become bright red like a brisk sunburn. It feels warm and itchy and

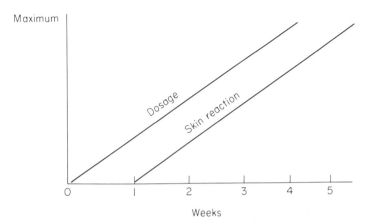

Figure 3. Skin reaction related to dosage.

is easily injured if scratched or rubbed. Hair, where this is included in the field, will begin to fall out. This is called epilation.

This is the degree of reaction at which the radiotherapist aims to finish the treatment course. It is one of the reasons for fractionation of dosage. It is also a reason for trying to avoid a break in the course once the treatment has begun. If we look at the skin reaction in relation to dosage on a graph, we see that the reaction lags behind the dose by about a week and reaches its peak after the course has been completed. A break in the treatment would allow it to catch up. To continue to treat on a brisk skin reaction should only be done under the direct supervision of the radiotherapist.

Once the treatment has been discontinued, the reaction fades and the skin becomes tanned. This takes about a week and it is followed by dry desquamation – peeling of the skin in dry flakes.

Third-degree erythema

A third-degree reaction is not much seen nowadays because of the skin-sparing effect of megavoltage radiation (see below). In certain situations, however, the skin-sparing effect is deliberately removed by use of bolus (tissue-equivalent materials) in order to bring the maximum dose up to the skin surface. In these situations the skin reaction will be much more marked and will require close attention. A third-degree reaction can, of course, be expected with low-energy radiation.

A third-degree erythema may follow on from a second-degree reaction after a course of treatment has been completed without further radiation being given – the reaction 'catches up'. If the treatment is continued on a brisk second-degree reaction, it will certainly appear and this entails risk. The skin becomes dark red or purplish. There is slight oedema and it feels tender to the touch. The skin is easily broken and blisters may form, with serum weeping from the raw areas. The patient feels ill and miserable.

THE EFFECT OF THE SKIN REACTION ON THE PATIENT

A brisk skin reaction probably adds to the patient's feeling of tiredness at the end of the course. This factor should be borne in mind when arrangements are to be made to send him to convalescence. If the convalescence can be delayed for a week to 10 days, the immediate reactions will have settled and the patient will derive more enjoyment and benefit from it. On a practical note also, many convalescent homes refuse to take patients who actually need nursing care.

LATE CHANGES IN THE SKIN

Late changes are related to:

Beam energy

The beam energy determines the part of the skin that is most affected by the radiation.

At low energy (up to 300 kV) the basal or germinal layer shows the most change. The cells are reduced in activity and the skin becomes thin and 'papery'. It is easily damaged and slow to heal. Epilation, except where the dose is too low to cause this, will be permanent. This is due to destruction of the hair follicles. The sweat glands are also destroyed. The superficial blood vessels may be severely damaged and obliterated. Other blood vessels enlarge to compensate, producing an unsightly condition called telangiectasis – a pale skin with enlarged red blood vessels. Injury to this skin may lead to necrosis.

High-energy radiation affects the subcutaneous layers. This is because, due to the forward scatter of the electrons with gamma radiation, the 100 per cent dose level (or build-up level) occurs at depths of 0.5 cm (cobalt 60) – 1 cm (6 MeV) under the skin surface. This phenomenon is called the skin-sparing effect.

The skin-sparing effect reduces the inflammatory reactions which occur on the skin at low energy, but fibrosis and scarring take place in the subcutaneous layers causing contraction and loss of elasticity. In severe cases this resembles pig skin and is known as leathering. Lymph channels are obliterated and the sweat glands cease to function. Hair follicles frequently survive or recover. In order to derive benefit from the skin-sparing effect, the irradiated skin must be uncovered during treatment, but reactions will occur in the flexures and creases in the skin. To overcome this, attempts should be made to open creases out. For example, in the treatment of a lesion of the pelvis, separating the legs will spare the skin of the groins by spreading the skin.

Although the patient suffers far less immediate discomfort from the acute reaction, he may suffer more from the late effects unless due care is taken. This is especially important in certain situations:
(1) When a lesion of a limb is irradiated to a high dose, fibrosis of the subcutaneous tissues will result in a tight inelastic band forming round the limb if the whole circumference is irradiated equally. This will cause pain and lymphoedema (oedema caused by disruption of lymphatic circulation) beyond the treated zone and even render the limb virtually useless. This may be avoided by leaving a strip of skin untreated along the length of the field to allow circulation of the lymph and some elasticity of the skin.
(2) When two fields are adjacent to each other, a gap must be left between them. The size of the gap depends on the beam energy and the depth of the 100 per cent build-up. Beam divergence causes overlap of the two fields under the skin. Unless a gap equal to twice the build-up depth is left, a dose of 200 per cent will be received under the skin at this depth (see Figure 4). The risk does not arise at lower energies.

Dosage and fractionation

High dosage produces marked changes in the skin. These changes are more severe if the dose is given in large fractions over a short time. The chances of a subsequent necrosis are also increased. Quite high dosage can be tolerated with minimal scarring if the treatment is given in smaller fractions over a slightly longer period. This is very important when the cosmetic effect is to be considered.

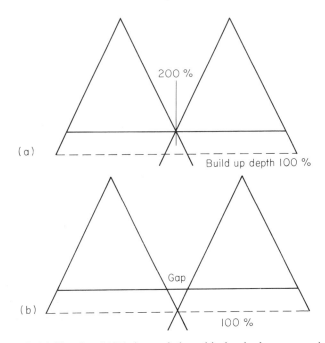

Figure 4. (a) Showing 200% dosage below skin level when no gap is allowed between fields; (b) gap equal to twice the build-up depth avoids overlap of beams below skin level.

Low dosage, especially at the lower energies, may cause abnormal mitoses in the germinal layer of the skin. Radiation-induced malignancy is a late risk in the treatment of non-malignant skin conditions by radiation, and is the reason for this practice being largely discontinued. The effect of small doses on the skin is cumulative.

METHODS OF SPARING THE SKIN

Apart from fractionation of dosage and the selection of a suitable beam energy described above, other means of sparing the skin include: multi-field techniques; beam-hardening filters; restriction of the area irradiated by cones and shielding. When lead is used for shielding at megavoltage, the blocks must be placed at least 15 cm from the skin. This distance allows the electrons generated in the lead to be lost in the air before reaching the skin.

CARE OF THE SKIN

Care of the skin during treatment is of great importance. If it is not cared for conscientiously, the course of treatment may have to be interrupted, with adverse effects on the patient's chances of a cure. It is the duty of the radiographer to advise and instruct the patient on the care of the skin and to ensure that the instructions are being followed. Instructions on skin care should be written down, but the patient should also have them carefully explained and be given the opportunity to ask questions.

On the first day of treatment instructions must be kept to a minimum because most patients have more than enough to think about, and are not very receptive! A detailed explanation on the following day will be better understood.

The radiographer must inspect the fields daily in a good light when the patient is on the couch. During this inspection there are two points to be borne in mind:

(1) How soon should the skin reaction be expected? This will depend on the conditions of treatment.

(2) Does the reaction, when it appears, match the dose which the skin has received? If the skin reaction appears too soon or is more brisk than expected, it is wise to seek a reason – is the dose correct? Are the physical factors correct? Is the patient following the instructions?

Washing

Hot water and soap must not be used on irradiated skin. They increase the blood supply to the site and make the reaction appear sooner than it might. However, patients must never be told not to wash. Cleanliness is essential for hygiene and comfort. Daily bathing in plain tepid water is particularly important for parts of the body where there is sweat or discharge from a wound or a body orifice. Patients undergong treatment to a pelvic organ must have a daily shallow tepid bath. This also reduces the risk of bladder infections in female patients. When perspiration is heavy, sodium bicarbonate may be added to the water in the proportion of 1 teaspoonful per pint.

A male patient must be given clear instructions with regard to shaving. He should not be allowed to use hot water. An electric razor may be used and he must be warned of the loss of the beard due to epilation.

The advantage of using tattoo marks to define the treatment area, or beam directional shells to carry the field marks, lies in the freedom from worry enjoyed by the patients about losing the marks.

Drying the skin

After washing, the skin should be dried by patting it with an absorbent towel. Friction must not be used as this also increases the blood supply to the site and may injure the skin if there is already a reaction. After drying, the skin is well powdered with a good talcum powder. Talcum powder prevents friction and absorbs moisture. The most suitable talcum powders are 'baby' powders, and these are recommended. Most good brand names are also suitable. Some brands contain zinc oxide. In the days of orthovoltage radiation this was of significance because electron scatter from the zinc increased the skin reaction, but with the skin-sparing effect of megavoltage radiation the effect is negligible.

Clothing

The patient is advised not to wear artificial fibres next to the skin. Man-made fibres do not absorb moisture and the risk of friction is therefore increased. Cotton (or silk) is to be preferred, especially for night wear. The clothing should not be too tight and cause pressure on the irradiated skin. Particular attention must be paid to shoulder-straps and brassieres when the chest wall and breast are treated. Friction can also be caused on the neck from jewellery and stiff collars. A man undergoing treatment for a tumour in the neck area should be advised to wear an open-neck shirt with a soft scarf or cravat rather than a collar and tie.

Other factors which increase the skin reaction

(1) Pressure from appliances such as spectacles (on the nose) or a supporting collar round the neck.

(2) Radiation and heat. Exposure of irradiated skin to the sun must be avoided. This precaution is continued long after the course of

treatment has finished. Local heat as a means of pain relief (hot water bottles or hot pads) must also be avoided.

(3) Infection. Infection devitalises the skin, causing poor tolerance and slow recovery. Pus and slough are anoxic and reduce the effect of radiation. Scabs and dried discharge act as bolus. They reduce the skin-sparing effect of high-energy radiation and the percentage depth dose at low energy.

(4) Drugs. When drugs are used to increase the sensitivity of the tissues to radiation, the skin reaction may also be more marked.

(5) Diabetic patients occasionally suffer marked skin reactions. By nature of their condition they are prone to sepsis, and wounds may be slow to heal.

(6) If a rash appears on the skin, especially in the early part of the course, the medical officer must be informed before irradiation is carried out.

Dressings in the irradiated area

A course of post-operative irradiation does not usually begin until the stitches have been removed and the wound is nearly healed. In most cases only a light protective dry dressing is required. Dressings should be removed during the treatment unless there are instructions to the contrary, because they affect the dose on the skin. In cases where the skin is broken, or the wound unhealed, it must be cleaned and a non-adhesive dressing applied. Painting the broken area with 2 per cent gentian violet solution is sometimes advised. Gentian violet is a bacteriostatic and fungicidal dye with slightly astringent properties. It should be allowed to dry on the skin and a light protective dressing applied to protect the clothing from the stain.

Dressings should be secured by a bandage rather than adhesive tape, to minimise the risk of skin damage. Conforming, tubular or Netelast bandage is easy to apply. Several types of adhesive tape available are suitable if used with care (e.g. Micropore). Zinc oxide strapping must never be used on skin to be irradiated. The zinc deposited in the skin increases the skin reaction markedly. The strapping is difficult to remove without skin damage. Sellotape should not be used either!

AFTERCARE OF THE SKIN

After the course of treatment is completed, the instructions regarding the care of the skin must be followed until the reactions have completely subsided and the skin has returned to 'normal'. This may not be for 3–4 weeks. After this period the skin must be treated gently – washing with warm water and mild soap. A little lanolin or good-quality skin cream may be applied to areas where dead skin is still adhering or the skin is very dry. Cream must not be applied while there is still any erythema. Sunbathing (or exposure to the sun) must be avoided for at least a year and then only with the advice of the radiotherapist.

TREATMENT OF THE BREAST AND CHEST WALL

Tumours of the breast are very common in women, the age of peak incidence being about 45. It is a tumour very rare in men. The treatment depends on the staging:

Stages 1 and 2 – surgery (mastectomy) followed by radiotherapy (unless the tumour is in the very early stages) to the chest wall and regional lymphatic areas.

Stage 3 – surgery is rarely possible because the tumour may be fixed to the chest wall and involve the skin. Radiotherapy is the most usual treatment.

Stage 4 – the disease has metastasised. Treatment is usually by radiotherapy supplemented by hormones and chemotherapy.

In the early stages the prognosis is good, becoming less so as the disease advances.

THE ACUTE REACTIONS

There is often oedema of the superficial tissues at the beginning of the treatment. This may add to the stiffness of the arm, but the reaction passes off quickly. The main reaction is that of the skin and this is often increased by:

(1)   tight clothing, especially brassiere, shoulder-straps, etc.

(2)   friction – coat collars (at the neck), artificial fiibres next to the skin, especially in the axilla and excessive movements of the arm;

(3)   warmth and moisture in the axilla;

(4)   sunburn on the front of the neck (in summer);

(5)   possible ulceration of the chest wall.

Most of these problems have been discussed in the section on the skin, and others will be enlarged on below.

Other reactions include:

(1)   Systemic: patients usually feel tired and depressed. Irradiation of the chest wall often causes nausea. Other causes of nausea in patients with breast carcinoma are hormone therapy, hypercalcaemia (raised blood calcium) due to bone metastases and liver involvement.

(2)   The blood: There will be a drop in the white cell count due to irradiation of the ribs and sternum.

(3)   Oesophagitis: the patient may complain of dysphagia (difficulty in swallowing) and dryness of the throat. This is due to a mucosal reaction in the upper oesophagus from the supra-clavicular field. Shielding the area will reduce this, though care must be taken not to shield the lymph nodes. Soft foods and fluids are advised. Aspirin will also help.

LATE RADIATION CHANGES

(1)   Fibrosis in the axilla is a late hazard, which is avoidable. This may be caused by overlap of the fields used to treat the axilla and chest wall. It may be due to bad planning or faulty positioning during the treatment. Axillary fibrosis causes intractable pain and lymphoedema of the arm due to blocking of the lymph drainage.

(2)   Bone: there may be changes in the head of the humerus and the ribs.

(3)   The heart: ischaemic changes have been noted in the heart tissues following irradiation of the left chest wall for a breast tumour. Ischaemia means reduction of blood supply.

(4)   The lungs: radiation pneumonitis may occur if the lung has been included in the irradiated zone. Irradiation of the lung is avoided by the use of tangential fields for the chest wall, but if these have a deep 'bite' or the beam has a large penumbra, some lung tissue may be included.

OTHER COMPLICATIONS

Lymphangitis

This is a rare complication which sometimes occurs after mastectomy. The patient complains of pain in the upper arm and the lymph vessels may be felt on the inner surface of the upper arm like hard cords. The medical officer must be informed and the patient advised to rest the arm; if need be in a sling.

CARE OF THE PATIENT

A mastectomy is a severe shock to a woman and every effort is made to lessen this by psychological preparation before the operation and by help to return to normality after it. One of the ways of achieving a return to normality is to disguise the fact that she has lost a breast. This is important for her own self-confidence and for her relationships with her family and friends.

The patient is fitted with a breast prosthesis (replacement part) as soon as practicable after the operation. A breast prosthesis is constructed to balance the normal breast for size and weight. If it is too heavy or too light, it will not hang properly and will look unbalanced. The best prostheses are made of rubber and contain cells filled with viscous fluid. Some are adjustable for size by adding or removing fluid. These feel like normal tissue.

A cheaper type of prosthesis is made of a bag containing small pellets. At one time it was recommended that lentils made a good filling, being of the correct weight for the volume!

A prosthesis is normally worn inside an ordinary brassiere by making a small pocket to hold it inside the cup. Several well-known makers of underwear specialise in manufacturing garments specifically for women who have had a mastectomy.

It may not always be advisable for the patient to wear a prosthesis during the course of irradiation, but a woman who is accustomed to the support of a brassiere will experience physical discomfort if this is denied her. She should be advised to wear one slightly larger than that to which she is accustomed and to place a large cotton handkerchief under it to cover the chest wall, pinning the handkerchief to the brassiere to keep it in place. Another folded handkerchief should be placed under the shoulder-strap in case of pressure.

If there are objections to the wearing of a prosthesis during the treatment period, the empty cup needs to be padded out to match the other side. For this, cotton wool should not be used; it soon becomes compacted and lumpy. It also retains heat and moisture. A more satisfactory alternative for a patient who is not too large is a sanitary towel pinned inside the brassiere and positioned so that it lies from the axilla downwards and medially across the chest wall. A second alternative is to fill the empty cup with crumpled handkerchiefs or cotton material. This allows the air to circulate and is cool to wear.

USE OF THE ARM

Following a mastectomy there may be difficulty and pain on using the arm. This is temporary, but the patient must be encouraged to use the arm and exercise it because there is a slight risk that the limitation of movement will become permanent. In some cases, physiotherapy is prescribed. Various exercises are recommended, including raising the arm over the head and brushing the hair. Another very good exercise is for the patient to extend the arm sideways, place the hand against a wall and 'walk' the fingers up as high as possible.

Many patients tend to stoop slightly towards the affected side. This is a protective measure and a simple corrective exercise is to practise walking upright.

ADVANCED DISEASE

From time to time patients present with very advanced breast tumours which are fungating (ulcerating and 'cauliflower-like'). These can be quite horrific. The smell is very offensive and the dead slough and infection make the tumour resistant to radiation.

Irradiation is used to reduce the tumour growth and prevent a haemorrhage which is likely to occur if the tumour erodes a vein. Oophorectomy (removal of the ovaries) and hormones also give good response in suitable patients. The ulcerated area must be cleaned up in order to: reduce the smell and ulceration; improve the response to treatment; spare the skin, which becomes very sore with the moisture and discharge.

Dressing for an ulcerated tumour

Requirements:
Dressing pack containing:

Gallipot.
Swabs.
Plain and toothed forceps – two pairs each.
Scissors.

Gauze swabs.
Ribbon gauze.

Also required:
Non-adhesive dressing (Vaseline gauze).
Wool pads and deodorant (Denodor) pads.
Eusol or hydrogen peroxide.
Water to reduce the lotion to half strength.
Netelast or conforming bandage.
Swab for culture.

The patient is placed supine on a couch and the surface of the couch
and the patient are protected by dressing towels. The area is cleansed
and any loose slough cut away. The ulcer may be packed with ribbon
gauze soaked in lotion and the area covered with a deodorant pad
with a wool pad on top.

If a swab is to be taken for culture, this must be done before the
ulcer is cleaned. This dressing must be done every day and if the
patient cannot do it for herself, arrangements must be made for her
to attend at the Casualty Department when the Radiotherapy
Department is closed, or for the district nurse to call.

Various deodorant devices are available through the pharmacy for
use in the treatment room while a patient with a fungating tumour is
being treated.

Lymphoedema of the arm is unsightly and disabling. It is not seen
as often as it used to be, mainly because most mastectomies are
'simple' mastectomy rather than 'radical', which involved the dissec-
tion of the lymph nodes in the axilla and interference with the lymph
drainage of the arm. With the advent of megavoltage, particularly
linear accelerators, the lymph drainage areas of the breast can be
more efficiently treated and therefore, in most cases, surgery is
limited to the removal of the breast only.

Lymphoedema may also be caused by axillary fibrosis, mentioned
above. This is an extremely serious condition and is irreversible. The
fibrosis may involve the brachial nerve, causing intractable pain with
loss of the use of the hand. Oedema of the arm may also be due to
metastatic disease of the axillary lymph nodes.

Some control of the swelling of the arm may be achieved by the
use of an elastic sleeve. This should be put on in the morning on rising, and removed at night. It should always be rolled from the wrist
upwards and never in the opposite direction. The patient is also
advised to raise the arm on a pillow at night. Physiotherapy may

sometimes be of help. The use of a 'Flowtron' air pump can also occasionally bring about an improvement. This creates pulsation in the limb which helps to improve lymph flow.

THE MUCOSA

The mucosa covers all parts of the body internally and is continuous with the skin at the body orifices. Like the skin it is an epithelial covering, but its structure varies from one part of the body to another and it contains specialised cells which secrete mucous.

THE EFFECTS OF RADIATION
ON THE MUCOSA

Radiation injures the mucosa in the same way as it injures the skin. The changes brought about may be seen in the mouth and throat when these areas are treated, but the same changes occur elsewhere – in the lung, bowel, bladder, etc., and the discomfort which the patient experiences in the area depends on the severity of the reaction. It is also important to note that, when treatment is given by megavoltage, the mucosal reaction occurs before the skin reaction because of the skin-sparing effect of high-energy radiation and the high percentage depth dose.

MUCOSAL REACTIONS

(1)   The first reaction on the mucosa is similar to a first-degree erythema of the skin and occurs at about the same dose level.

(a) There will be slight reddening of the area irradiated.

(b) There will be an increase in the secretions – for example increased salivation in the mouth.

(c) In some cases there will be slight oedema. This only occurs at the beginning of treatment, but it may be significant. A large tumour of the larynx or bronchus may partly obstruct the airway, and oedema caused by radiation may make the situation worse. If a patient exhibits signs of stridor (noisy breathing) after the first or second dose of radiation, he must be seen by the medical officer before further treatment is given. When oedema is likely to occur, the dangers are minimised by beginning with fairly small dosage fractions and increasing over a few days to the full dose.

(2)   As the treatment progresses the mucosal surfaces become markedly reddened and the patient begins to experience discomfort. This stage is reached at about 2000 cGy on megavoltage. The type of discomfort depends on the part of the body irradiated:

   in the mouth – dryness and loss of taste;
   in the chest – a cough and dysphagia;
   in the pelvis – diarrhoea and cystitis.

The risk of infection in the irradiated area is high because the natural protective flora are reduced by the radiation, the mucosa is inflamed and the secretions are reduced.

(3)   From 3500 cGy onwards a fibrinous or membranous reaction may be expected. Patches of white fibrin or membrane appear on the irradiated mucosa. If these are removed or disturbed, the mucosal surface will bleed. At this stage the patient is seen frequently by the radiotherapist, especially when the mouth and throat are being treated.

(4)   The white fibrin becomes yellow and separates, leaving a red, sore surface. This stage is reached at a dose level of 5000–6000 cGy, and at this point the course of treatment is complete.

LATE CHANGES

The mucosa heals fairly rapidly once treatment is discontinued. High dosage is followed by scarring and fibrous changes in the mucosa. This will take the form of:

(1)   smoothness and loss of texture of the mucosal surface;
(2)   paleness due to reduced blood supply caused by fibrosis of the smaller blood vessels;
(3)   loss of elasticity and shrinkage;
(4)   loss of secretions due to fibrosis of the secreting cells.

   These changes are not without their effect on the patient, who must in the long term learn to live with them.

   Every effort is made to reduce the effects of radiation by:

(1)   planning and choice of field arrangement to spare the normal mucosa when possible;
(2)   shielding of vital structures such as the lung, kidney and salivary glands, etc.;
(3)   dosage fractionation for tissue tolerance;
(4)   choice of beam energy or method of treatment;
(5)   prevention and treatment of infection;
(6)   care of the reactions by use of specific remedies, diet, rest and fluid intake.

IRRADIATION OF THE MOUTH AND THROAT

The mucosal reaction is the most important factor in the treatment of the respiratory tract and the alimentary tract. The upper respiratory and alimentary tracts are the sites of many tumours which are treated by irradiation. Radiotherapy is the treatment of choice because of the mutilation and loss of function which would follow radical surgery. Megavoltage is essential for tissue-sparing, especially bone in the face and the cartilage of the larynx. Hyperbaric oxygen may be used for resistant tumours in conjunction with the radiation.

Patient care is of very great importance when the mouth and throat are irradiated, and may make all the difference between success and failure in the completion of the course. It is essential to gain the patient's co-operation. This is done by clear explanation of what is to be done and what he is to expect. Before treatment begins, certain preparations have to be made to improve the likelihood of treatment success.

PRE-TREATMENT CARE

Infection

Prior to irradiation of the mouth, dental inspection is carried out and treatment is given for infected teeth if necessary. Bad teeth are likely to contribute to poor physical condition through pain and sepsis. Chest infections may also be of significance. These are investigated and treated. If the patient smokes, he is advised to give it up or reduce the habit. This becomes more important when the radiation reaction begins to develop on the treated mucosa. He is also advised to avoid places where he is likely to come into contact with tobacco smoke and respiratory infections for the duration of his treatment. This in itself may be a good enough reason for allowing hospital transport rather than asking him to travel by public transport if he lives at a distance.

Diet

Not all patients are in a poor physical condition when they first present for treatment. On the other hand, those that are may be in a very poor state indeed. A tumour in the upper oesphagus causing difficulty in eating or swallowing, perhaps over a period of time, brings about a state of chronic malnutrition with severe weight loss and anaemia. Chronic anaemia as a result of poor nutrition causes 'webbing' or sagging of the pharyngeal tissues. This in turn gives rise to dysphagia (difficulty in swallowing) and is associated with lesions of the upper oesophagus. Patients are most likely to be elderly women of poor social background. This is known as Plummer Vinson or Patterson Kelly syndrome. Anaemia must be corrected before treatment is begun and a blood transfusion is the most effective method in a short time. A high-protein diet will improve the patient's general state. If swallowing is difficult, feeding by nasogastric tube may be necessary.

Background care

Poor physical condition is usually associated with poor social conditions. A patient in good social circumstances rarely reaches an advanced state of disease before seeking medical advice. A full course of radiotherapy for a lesion of the mouth or throat is a trying experience, and the patient needs help and support. Even when his family are co-operative, the medical social worker can offer valuable help and advice and the assistance of the dietician is also invaluable, especially towards the end of the course.

CARE DURING TREATMENT

The mucosal reaction is the reaction from which the patient will have most discomfort. This can be very uncomfortable indeed but the discomfort can be minimised by proper care:

Oral hygiene

This is of vital importance for two reasons:
(1)   to reduce the risk of infection;
(2)   to enable the patient to eat with ease.

Irradiation of the buccal mucosal destroys much of the natural protective flora and opens the way to infective organisms. The mouth and teeth should be cleaned regularly both before and after meals with a soft toothbrush. A baby's toothbrush is ideal. In addition, mouth-washes are used. These are bacteriostatic and they make the mouth feel fresh and moist. Any of the three listed below are suitable:

potassium chlorate;

glyco-thymol;

sodium bicarbonate and boracic in the proportion of 1 teaspoonful of each to a pint of tepid water. This may be made up by the patient as required.

If hygiene is neglected, infection is almost certain. The most likely infection is thrush (*Candida albicans*) which grows on the mucosa. It appears quite quickly and causes extreme soreness and discomfort. In appearance it resembles a white fibrinous reaction, but it must not be confused with this. The speed at which it appears, and the fact that it is not confined solely to the treated area but may be spread all over the buccal surface, should be clues to its diagnosis. Its appearance also is not dependent on dosage level. It may be present when the dose is quite low. A further difference is that the white patches cannot be removed in the way that fibrinous patches can be removed. If thrush is suspected, further irradiation should not be given until the patient has been seen by a medical officer. To continue is to risk severe mucosal damage. A fungicidal preparation such as nystatin will be prescribed. This is used in the form of a suspension to be held in the mouth, 1 ml four times per day. Strict oral hygiene is also initiated.

Diet

Once the mucosal reaction appears, loss of taste and dryness of the mouth reduce the desire to eat. It is, however, important to the maintenance of the patient's general condition that he should take adequate food and not feel hungry. When necessary, the dietician will give advice and help to the patient or his family.

It may be necessary in some cases to admit the patient towards the end of the course if he has a poor home background or if he cannot cope with suitable meals. During the course of treatment it is advisable to keep a record of his weight. Weight loss may indicate inadequate nourishment. The diet itself should be high in protein and easily swallowed. It must not be entirely fluid because it is difficult to get enough nourishment from fluids only without taking a very large quantity, and the patient will feel unsatisfied without some solids. The diet should include:

Milk, either on its own or used in drinks, puddings and custards.
Eggs, soft boiled, scrambled or beaten into milk.

Soups, especially those made from pulses (beans, peas).

Fish, and minced meat of all kinds.

Cheese, especially soft cheese and yoghurt.

Soft fresh fruit (pears, bananas, grapes, melon etc.) and fresh orange or tomato juice daily to supply vitamin C.

Protein supplements such as Complan may be given if it is thought necessary, but are not essential if a proper diet is followed. Vitamins and iron may also be prescribed, but again these are present in a balanced diet.

An old-fashioned 'radiotherapy' diet which is very pleasant and very nourishing is Palmasteria's diet. It is not intended that this should be the patient's whole food intake, but it is a basic source of calories and fat-soluble vitamins. The calorie value is 1100 per litre. The average patient needs about 1800 calories per day. Palmasteria's diet is as follows:

1 litre milk;

30 g wheat flour;

20 g glucose;

40 g of butter;

1 egg.

Blend all the ingredients and cook in a double saucepan to a custard. Brandy in the proportion of 1 part to 10 parts may be added if liked, or any other flavouring according to taste.

All food should be taken warm rather than hot and the seasoning should be reduced, especially salt and spices as these will 'sting' a raw surface. Cold or iced drinks will be found acceptable when the mouth is sore and dry.

Medication

Medication, in the form of a mild anaesthetic, will help to reduce the discomfort of a severe mucosal reaction and make it easier for the patient to eat. This will be prescribed towards the end of the course and immediately following its completion. Aspirin mucilage and mucaine are both jelly-like preparations which coat the surfaces when held in the mouth. They may be rinsed out or swallowed. Equally effective is one soluble aspirin dissolved in $\frac{1}{2}$ teacup of warm water and used as a mouth-wash or gargle. In cases of digestive disorders, where aspirin may be contraindicated, these preparations may still be used provided that the patient does not swallow them.

Resting the affected part

This is advisable, especially when the mucosal reaction appears. Talking should be reduced to a minimum. This is important when the larynx is irradiated in order to rest the vocal cords.

Regular inspection

Regular inspection of the mouth and throat is carried out by the medical officer. These inspections are at weekly intervals or more frequently if it is thought necessary. The reasons for inspection are:
(1)   assessment of the tumour response;
(2)   possible infection in the irradiated area;
(3)   assessment of local reactions.

Irradiation of the mouth and throat causes little or no change in the white blood count as a general rule. In some cases only, e.g. lymphosarcoma, the blood count will have to be monitored.

Late changes

The mucosa

Fibrosis and loss of vascularity in the mucosa will cause dryness and loss of taste which will persist for a long time and may be permanent. This is something to which the patient adjusts in time.

Salivary glands

Damage to the salivary glands causes loss of the secretions and makes a big difference in the moistness of the mouth. At least some of the glands must be spared whenever possible by planning, shielding and by using a bite block during the treatment to separate the jaws and enable part of the mouth to be spared. Artificial saliva preparations are available on prescription. These are taken into the mouth before meals and as required to replace the natural secretion when it has been completely inhibited.

The teeth

Decreased salivation and alteration of the acidity of the mouth as a result of irradiation increases the risk of dental caries. There may also be some changes in the bone of the jaw and reduction of the blood supply to the teeth. The patient is always advised to inform his dentist that he has had a course of irradiation before any extractions are done, because there is a risk of haemorrhage.

TRACHEOSTOMY

A tracheostomy is an opening into the trachea via the front of the neck, made necessary by an obstruction of the airway due to a tumour or following surgery for the removal of the larynx (laryngectomy). The opening or 'stoma', is kept patent by means of a metal tube which is held in place by tapes around the neck. The opening is protected in front by an 'apron' of gauze and/or a metal shield. A patient with a tracheostomy is at some risk as far as chest infections are concerned because he does not have the bacterial trap of the mouth, and throat and nasal passages, before the air enters the lungs.

Secondly, the air which enters via the stoma is not warmed and moistened as it would be by passing through the mouth and nose. In order to compensate for this, the gauze apron is kept moist. This, however, has its own disadvantages in that:
(1)   it may make the skin sore, especially if it is in the irradiated area;
(2)   it can easily become the source of bacterial infection if it is not changed regularly.

Patients who are to receive radiation therapy will have the metal tube changed for a plastic one so that electron scatter from the metal will not add to the dose at the site. Initially this may make the patient a bit nervous and insecure because he will miss the weight of the metal tube. A plastic one is lighter and easy to dislodge.

A patient with a tracheostomy has difficulty (at least initially) in clearing the sputum from the trachea and the stoma, and has to be assisted by medical suction. Suction can be compared to a vacuum cleaner. It is an operation which makes many students feel squeamish, but one has to overcome this feeling and remember that it is far more unpleasant for a patient who feels he is going to suffocate.

The apparatus

The apparatus for medical suction consists of an electric motor operating a suction pump which draws air out of a glass bottle via

Tube A in Figure 5. As the bottle is pumped out, more air or any fluid or sputum is drawn into it via Tube B. The bottle contains a small amount of antiseptic solution so that any infected material is rendered safe. Some modern hospitals have medical suction available as a service in all clinical rooms.

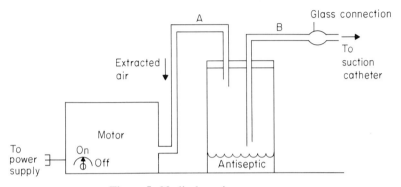

Figure 5. Medical suction apparatus.

The equipment for medical suction

Suction equipment, plugged in and ready for use.
Glass connection.
Suction catheters; these are pre-packed and sterile.
Sterile forceps.
Sterile water in a sterile container.
Disposal bags.

Method

Fit the catheter to suction Tube B via the glass connection.
   Switch on the motor.
   Using the right hand, hold the catheter about half-way along its length with the forceps. Support the suction tube in the left hand. Gently introduce the catheter into the stoma, clearing the entrance. When the catheter is inside, pinch the suction tube to cut off the suction. This builds up the vacuum in the bottle. Withdraw the catheter, and as it is being withdrawn, release the tube pressure. By releasing pressure on the tube the force of suction is momentarily increased and this will clear the airway. It is very important that this method of increasing the suction force should only be used when the

catheter is being withdrawn – i.e. stop the suction as the catheter is being introduced, suck as it is being withdrawn. To increase suction as it is being introduced may result in matter being carried into the trachea and thence into the lung.

The catheter is cleared between each suction by drawing sterile water through it. After use, the catheter is disposed of, the bottle emptied and cleaned and the equipment reassembled and tested.

IRRADIATION OF INTRATHORACIC TUMOURS

A major factor which governs the planning and treatment of a thoracic lesion is the tolerance of the lung. The lung is sensitive to radiation and late fibrotic changes will impair the quality of the patient's life. The thoracic organs are the site of many tumours.

The lung

(1)   Primary tumours of the lung are common. Most early tumours of the lung are treated by surgery (pneumonectomy or lobectomy), but a large percentage of patients do not come for treatment until the disease has spread to the mediastinal lymph nodes, or to the liver and bone.

(2)   Secondary malignant disease – many tumours metastasise to the lungs via the blood (breast, bone tumours and testicular tumours). In some cases a single round 'cannonball' metastasis (a well-rounded deposit characteristic of kidney tumours) may be removed surgically, provided it is proven to be the only one present by whole lung tomography. (Tomography is a diagnostic X-ray technique by which a part of the body is radiographed in layers). Otherwise, secondary lung disease is treated by chemotherapy.

The mediastinum

The thorax contains a large amount of lymphatic tissue. The mediastinal nodes are a common site for malignant disease, especially lymphomas such as Hodgkin's disease. The lung drains to the mediastinal nodes and they will therefore become the site of secondary involvement from a lung tumour.

The oesophagus

Radiotherapy is the treatment of choice for tumours of the middle third of the oesophagus. Surgery is possible but it involves a major operation and most of the patients presenting for treatment are in a very poor physical state. Excellent results are obtainable from irradiation of the oesophagus, but unless it is carefully planned and carried out, the side-effects may cancel them out. The oesophagus is a site particularly well suited to the computerised techniques currently being developed in radiotherapy.

The thyroid

Tumours of the thyroid which are operable are removed surgically (thyroidectomy). Certain tumours (follicular and papillary) take up iodine and are treated by I^{131}. Other inoperable tumours are treated by external irradiation.

THE ACUTE REACTIONS

The lung

The acute radiation reaction in the lung is not unlike pneumonia and is called radiation pneumonitis. There is an inflammatory reaction in the irradiated zone with an exudate in the tissues. This reaction appears at a dose level of from 2000 to 2500 cGy megavoltage. In some cases the patient has no symptoms. Some patients complain of a slight cough. In other cases, symptoms appear 2–3 weeks after the completion of the course of treatment. These take the form of a dry cough, breathlessness and a raised temperature. An X-ray film will reveal shadowing in the irradiated zone. The condition responds to cortisone and antibiotics, but the treatment must be prompt and effective to avoid the risk of lung fibrosis later on.

The oesophagus

Irradiation of the oesophagus causes dysphagia and discomfort on swallowing. The patient may complain of a 'lump' or a feeling of indigestion.

The mediastinum

A mediastinal reaction does not usually occur during the irradiation of a lung tumour or even of a mediastinal tumour unless the dose is very high. It may occur as a result of a perforation of the oesophagus

– for instance an oesophageal tumour may erode the wall or the shrinkage of a tumour in the oesophagus may leave a hole and the food will pass into the mediastinum. A mediastinal reaction is likely to occur during the treatment of a thymic tumour. The reaction is characterised by retrosternal pain and a raised pulse. When the reaction is suspected, treatment should be withheld until the patient has been seen by a doctor.

Other reactions

Other reactions which occur on irradiation of a thoracic lesion are: the skin; the blood count; the systemic reaction.

LATE RADIATION CHANGES

The lung

About 6–12 months after irradiation there will be fibrosis of the irradiated zone. This will be visible on an X-ray film. The fibrosis causes shrinkage of the tissues and if a large area of lung is involved this will cause:
(1)   breathlessness due to non-functioning lung;
(2)   displacement of the intrathoracic contents which in turn gives rise to cardiac and other symptoms.

The heart

It is generally assumed that the heart is resistant to radiation. It is an organ which is often included at least partly in the field. E.C.G. (electrocardiograph) investigations carried out on patients who have had radiotherapy for thoracic and breast tumours have shown that some changes do take place. A dose of 3000 cGy may cause ischaemic changes, the changes becoming apparent about 12 months after irradiation. It is believed that this increases the risk of cardiac arrest at a later date.

The oesophagus

A high dose of radiation to the oesophagus causes fibrosis and narrowing of the lumen. This follows irradiation of the oesophagus as a primary site but not usually when it is in the field of treatment of another lesion. When the patient suffers inconvenience from dysphagia, the oesophagus may be dilated under anaesthetic.

METHODS OF SPARING THE LUNGS

(1) Planning to spare the lung as much as possible by suitable field arrangement.

(2) The use of high-energy radiation for tissue-sparing and a well-defined beam with long S.S.D. (source–skin distance).

(3) Treatment of chest wall lesions by tangential fields.

(4) Lead shielding of the lungs during the treatment of mediastinal lesions – for example Mantle technique.

(5) Computerised techniques for sites such as the oesophagus. In this technique the radiation field is shaped to the lesion, with greater sparing of the surrounding tissues.

(6) Chemotherapy for the treatment of secondary disease of the lung.

(7) Care of the patient and treatment of the reactions.

CARE OF THE PATIENT

The care of the patient who is to undergo irradiation of an intrathoracic lesion falls into two parts:.

Pre-treatment care

This is important because it helps to prepare the patient to stand the treatment and to derive maximum benefit from it. It includes:

Correction of anaemia

This is of particular importance in treatment of tumours of the oesophagus where long-standing dysphagia may have brought about a state of near-starvation in the patient. Tumours of the lung and advanced tumours of the breast also cause general malaise and loss of appetite, which in turn causes weight loss and under-nourishment.

Infection

The lung is a common site for infection. The early diagnosis of lung tumours is often made difficult by such concurrent infections as bronchitis and 'smoker's cough', etc. Sputum tests are done to exclude infection and suitable antibiotics prescribed as required.

Patients with chronic bronchitis combined with a lung tumour present a special problem for the radiotherapist and generally have a poor prognosis. Chronic bronchitis usually results in emphysema – rupture of the alveolar walls with consequent reduction in the efficiency of gas exchange in the lungs. The patient becomes cyanosed and dyspnoeic on even minimal exertion, and needs oxygen frequently. Radiation fibrosis in the irradiated zone reduces the lung function still further. Throughout the treatment, every effort is made to reduce the risk of concurrent infection. Hygiene is important in the treatment room and the patient is advised to avoid places where the risk of infection is high – crowds, places of entertainment etc. – for the duration of his treatment, especially in winter. Here also, as in the case of mouth and throat irradiation, there is good reason for allowing him to be brought to hospital by ambulance rather than by public transport.

Care of the patient during the treatment

A cough which is troublesome may be treated by a cough-suppressant linctus. This is especially helpful at night if the patient cannot get uninterrupted sleep. A linctus must always be prescribed by the medical officer. The patient should never be told to buy one from a chemist.

A cough-suppressant linctus stops the cough. When the cough is due to infection or the presence of sputum it will do nothing to get rid of the cause and may even be harmful. If the patient has a 'productive cough', i.e. is bringing up sputum, the sputum should be investigated for bacteria. It will also be helpful if an expectorant linctus is prescribed. This will loosen the material in the lungs and help to get rid of it. Pain is controlled by analgesia as required.

Dysphagia due to an oesophageal reaction is treated by a soft, easily swallowed diet, and by aspirin preparations such as:
(1) aspirin mucilage;
(2) a soluble aspirin dissolved in water and swallowed before meals.

Dysphagia is also helped by iced water, sipped slowly before meals. This is safer than aspirin and the cold acts as a mild analgesic.

Diet

The patient needs a light, nourishing diet with plenty of fluids. Weight loss is common with lung disease and the diet should therefore contain carbohydrates, proteins and fats. a record of the patient's weight should be kept during the course of the treatment. Weight loss is an adverse sign in the treatment of lung tumours. Anti-emetics and vitamins are prescribed as required.

Regular inspection

The patient must be seen at regular intervals by the medical officer during the course of treatment. In the case of large lung tumours, a chest X-ray is done about mid-way through the course and the response of the tumour assessed, with a view to reducing the volume treated and thereby sparing lung tissue.

IRRADIATION OF THE ABDOMINAL ALIMENTARY TRACT AND PELVIS

Irradiation of an organ in the abdominal or pelvic cavity must result in some radiation being delivered to a part of the alimentary tract. The reactions of the alimentary tract are a limiting factor in the treatment of abdominal lesions, particularly when the volume is large. Abdominal organs treated by radiation include:

(1)   The para-aortic and pelvic lymph nodes in Hodgkin's disease and testicular tumours. The field is large and shaped like an inverted Y. The treatment volume is carefully localised by lymphangiogram and the field limited by lead shielding.

(2)   Kidney tumours may be irradiated post-operatively.

(3)   The tumours which are most often treated by irradiation are those of organs of the pelvic cavity – bladder, cervix, uterus and rectum – and the reactions of these organs and of the large bowel are important.

(4)   The alimentary tract itself is not, with the exception of the rectum, a suitable site for irradiation as a primary means of treatment. This is because:

(a) it is accessible to surgery;

(b) there is too much mobility for accurate localisation of a tumour and immobilisation during treatment;

(c) the severe radiation reactions would have an adverse effect on the patient;

(d) Tumours of the gut are fairly radio-resistant.

Reactions in other abdominal organs are discussed below (the kidneys, bladder and the reproductive system).

BARIUM

Barium sulphate is used to investigate the alimentary tract, either by a barium meal or barium enema. Barium is a heavy metal and any residue of barium in the bowel during irradiation will increase the mucosal reaction by electron scatter. A mild aperient, preferably an oily one, should be given to remove the barium when it is present prior to starting a course of radiation treatment.

THE ACUTE REACTION

The acute reactions must be discussed under three headings:

The small bowel

The small bowel has a low tolerance of radiation. A dose of 2000–2500 cGy may cause a severe reaction with the risk of permanent damage. For this reason it is never deliberately irradiated to a high dose. However, it may happen that a loop of small bowel low in the pelvis is included in the field of radiation during the treatment of a pelvic tumour, or the pelvic fields may extend further up than is normal. The small bowel is part of the alimentary tract in which much of the process of digestion and assimilation of food takes place. The contents are very fluid and an inflammatory reaction in this part causes:
(1)   Severe colic (pain) with wind and 'gurgling' in the gut.
(2)   Very fluid diarrhoea, over which the patient has no control. If this continues it leads to dehydration and loss of food and vitamins (avitaminosis). The effect is in fact very similar to a small bowel infection and the patient becomes very ill.

The large bowel

The section of the large bowel in the pelvis is often irradiated during the treatment of a tumour of a pelvic organ and a radiation reaction causes inflammation of the bowel lining with diarrhoea and frequency of motions. If the reaction is severe, there will be passage of slime and blood.

Although there is no risk of loss of nourishment as with the small bowel, the patient will suffer great discomfort and misery if the reaction is not controlled. In severe reactions there is the risk of permanent damage and obstruction due to adhesions.

The rectum

The acute reaction in the rectum causes diarrhoea with slime and blood if severe. A characteristic of the rectal reaction is a sharp knife-like pain on passing a motion. This is called tenesmus. A radiation reaction of the rectum is called radiation proctitis, and if the rectum is over-irradiated this may become chronic. There is also a risk of necrosis.

CARE OF THE ACUTE REACTIONS

Minimising the bowel reaction is essential for patient comfort and successful treatment.

The bowel is spared by keeping the dose fractionation within tolerance. As a general rule the maximum dose is 1000 cGy per week. The position of the rectum is ascertained during the localisation procedure for other organs and its position shown on the plan. In the calculation of the dose distribution, that received by the rectum must be noted.

Diet

A low-residue diet is prescribed for patients undergoing irradiation of the abdominal or pelvic organs. The purpose of the diet is to rest the bowel as much as possible. A low-residue diet entails the avoidance of all 'roughage'.

The following items are not permitted:

Brown or wholemeal bread or items made with wholemeal flour.
Porridge oats or breakfast cereals.
Uncooked green vegetables, salads or fruit.
Whole beans, peas and fibrous vegetables or fruit (turnips, carrots, plums etc.) and dried fruit.
Oily fish and fatty meats.

Very small amounts of the following are allowed:

Bananas, sieved vegetables and stewed fruit.

A normal amount of the following is allowed:

Lean meat and white fish.
Cheese and eggs.

White bread and items made with white flour.
Potatoes, boiled or mashed.
Carbohydrates such as rice, semolina, etc., and milk puddings.

A daily supply of fresh strained fruit juice (orange, grapefruit, etc.) or tomato juice or bottled juices such as blackcurrant or apple is essential for the supply of vitamin C. The daily fluid intake should be increased. Vitamin tablets are prescribed.

This may seem a rather stodgy diet, but it only needs to be maintained for the duration of the course of treatment and it adds greatly to the patient's comfort.

Specific remedies

It is essential that the radiographer should ask the patient about the bowel action. Many patients do not like to talk about it, but there is a risk of bowel damage if diarrhoea goes undetected. Anti-diarrhoeals are prescribed as required, and in severe cases the treatment may be temporarily suspended at the discretion of the medical officer.

LATE CHANGES

Small bowel

The late radiation changes in the small bowel are due to fibrosis. The severity of the effect depends on the length of the bowel affected and the dose to which it was irradiated. Fibrosis causes narrowing of the lumen of the gut, malabsorption of food, and avitaminosis. There may be obstruction due to adhesions if the reactions were severe and the only remedy is surgery.

Large bowel

There will be narrowing of the gut due to fibrosis and the loss of peristasis. This gives rise to chronic constipation with which the patient learns to live. It is corrected by diet and by mild laxatives such as Milpar.

Rectum

Fibrosis in the rectum, as in the large bowel, will cause constipation. A more serious late radiation risk is possible necrosis of the anterior wall. This is avoidable with proper care.

A necrosis of the anterior rectal wall in a woman will cause a rectovaginal fistula – an opening between the rectum and the vagina. This enables the rectal contents to pass out via the vagina, with no control and a high risk of infection in the bladder and cervix.

In a man, the bladder lies in front of the rectum and a vesico-rectal fistula would allow the rectal contents to enter the bladder.

COLOSTOMY

Excision of the rectum for the removal of a tumour is a curative procedure. The operation known as S.C.A.P.E.R. (semi-circular antero-posterior excision of rectum). The colon is brought out onto the abdominal wall on the left-hand side. This is called a colostomy. In some cases a temporary colostomy may be done to bypass the rectum and anal canal in the course of treating a tumour of the anal canal by radioactive implant. Following an excision of the rectum, it is of course permanent.

The opening of the colostomy is carefully placed to avoid creases in the skin and it is covered by a waterproof bag to receive the faeces. The bag has an adhesive surface at the top which sticks to the skin and seals the opening. The hole in the adhesive part of the bag must be cut to the correct size before the cover of the adhesive part is removed, and the bag carefully placed so that it covers the stoma and does not stick to the mucosa of the bowel. If this is not done properly it will cause leakage of the faeces, excoriated skin and misery for the patient. When a patient with a colostomy undergoes a course of radiotherapy to the abdomen, the stoma is shielded or avoided and extra care must be taken to minimise the bowel reactions. Although some patients manage to achieve a degree of control over their bowel movements, they have not got the control of the rectum and the anal sphincter.

THE REPRODUCTIVE SYSTEM

The ovaries and the testes are very sensitive to the effects of radiation. Quite small doses will inhibit or destroy their function. Care must be taken to avoid irradiation of the gonads of children and young people of childbearing age.

The testes

Testicular tumours are removed surgically, the incision being made in the groin to avoid the necessity of subsequent irradiation of the scrotum. Post-operative irradiation is given to the para-aortic lymph nodes. The mediastinum and supraclavicular lymph nodes may also be irradiated, depending on the extent of the disease.

The ovaries

Tumours of the ovaries are not usually irradiated because of the large volume to be treated and the reactions in the gut. Surgery and/or chemotherapy are the treatments of choice.

The corpus uteri

Malignant tumours may be irradiated post-operatively if the pelvic lymphatics are involved, or the disease is infiltrating the muscle.

The cervix uteri

Malignant disease of the cervix uteri is very common. The treatment of choice for an early tumour (Stage I) is intra-cavitary irradiation followed by surgery. The later stages (Stages 2 and 3) are treated by intra-cavitary irradiation supplemented by external radiation (megavoltage) to the whole pelvis.

Pre-treatment care

Prior to treatment of a tumour of the cervix uteri, pre-treatment care of the patient includes:
(1) Correction of anaemia. Vaginal bleeding is a presenting symptom of tumours of the cervix uteri. If this has continued for any length of time, the patient may be very anaemic.
(2) Treatment of infection. The cervix and vagina are very common sites of infection – *E. coli*, V.D., thrush, herpes. An old injury possibly incurred at childbirth, or even as a result of a speculum examination, may be the cause of a long-standing low-grade infection. The patient may have a poor standard of hygiene. A low-grade infection can bring about erosion of the mucosal surface and cause a discharge. A white bloodless discharge is called leukorrhoea.

An effective method of treating a cervix infection is douching. It is a procedure which the patient may learn to do for herself at home and the equipment can be borrowed from the hospital.

Requirements for a vaginal douche

This is not an aseptic procedure, but the equipment should be sterile.
(1) Mackintosh or waterproof cover for the couch.
(2) Warmed bedpan.
(3) Douche can.
(4) Tubing and douche nozzle or Jaques' catheter.
(5) Bowl of Savlon to cleanse the perineal area.
(6) Cotton-wool swabs.
(7) 2 pint measure containing 2 pints of sodium bicarbonate solution of the strength of 1 teaspoonful of sodium bicarbonate to 1 pint of warm water.
(8) Sterile plastic gloves for the operator.
(9) Sanitary towel.
(10) Disposal bag.
   The water should be purified water, warmed by standing the bottle in a container of hot water, or alternatively, cooled boiled tap water.

Method

(1) Protect the bed.
(2) Place the patient supine on the bed with the bed pan under her and her head fairly low.
(3) Swab the perineal area.
(4) Connect the tubing and catheter to the douche can. Clip or kink the tubing and fill the can.
(5) Allow a little fluid to run through to expel the air from the tubing.
(6) Insert the catheter gently into the vagina and allow the fluid to run in and irrigate it. Raise the can a little, but not too high or the pressure will be too great, and force infected material up the canal. When the can is empty, dry the patient and give her a sanitary towel.

The acute reactions

Initially there will be vaginitis and discharge. The discharge becomes less as the secretions diminish.

Late changes

Fibrosis and loss of secretions in the vagina. Radiation menopause. Ablation of ovarian function occurs with doses of about 1000 cGy.

Radiation ablation of the ovaries is sometimes carried out on women suffering from excessively heavy menopausal bleeding to bring about the menopause. It is thought that there is a late risk of malignant change occurring in the corpus uteri following this form of treatment.

THE RENAL TRACT

The kidneys

The kidneys have a low tolerance of radiation. A dose in excess of 2000 cGy megavoltage is likely to cause late fibrosis and functional failure. When the kidneys are in the proximity of an irradiated zone – for instance in a lower Mantle technique for the treatment of Hodgkin's disease or a testicular tumour – they are localised by intravenous urography at the planning stage and shielded.

When the whole abdomen is irradiated, as may be the case in malignant peritoneal disease, the kidneys are shielded at a dose level of 1800 cGy. This is a slightly lower dose level than tolerance allows for scattered radiation in the treatment zone.

The bladder

The bladder is a primary target for radiation therapy and the treatment is a curative measure for malignant tumours. External radiation by megavoltage is used for invasive tumours. Papillary carcinomata may be treated by gold seed implant unless the tumour is close to the trigone, where radiation fibrosis will damage the ureters.

Pre-treatment care

Pre-treatment care of patients with bladder lesions includes:
(1) Correction of anaemia. Haematuria (passing blood in the urine) is a presenting symptom and many patients are anaemic.
(2) Treatment of infection. A C.V.S.U. is obtained for investigation and antibiotics prescribed as required.

THE ACUTE REACTIONS

Reactions begin to appear at a dose level of about 3000 cGy. Radiation cystitis (inflammation) may cause dysuria (burning and difficulty on passing urine) and frequency of micturition. This may cause great distress.

CARE OF THE REACTIONS

Increased fluid intake helps to alleviate the discomfort, although the patient may be disinclined to drink much because of the frequency. He should be encouraged to do so. Suitable medication is prescribed. The risk of infection must be borne in mind. Cystitis, with symptoms similar to those caused by the radiation, may occur.

A patient with severe dysuria may have to be catheterised. This is not desirable because of the risk of irritating the bladder and introducing infection. Male patients may be supplied with an external appliance consisting of a sheath which fits over the penis and supported by a strap around the waist. The sheath ends in a catheter and a urine collection bag.

LATE CHANGES

Late radiation fibrosis of the bladder causes shrinkage and loss of elasticity and capacity. Radiation dosage to the pelvis must not exceed 6000 cGy in 6 weeks because there will be a risk of pelvic fibrosis (frozen pelvis).

IRRADIATION OF BONE

The bones are frequently irradiated during the treatment of other unrelated tumours because they are in the path of the beam – for example, the pelvic bones, the skull and the ribs. The amounts absorbed at various energies is shown in Figure 6.

PRIMARY BONE TUMOURS

These are not very common:
(1) Osteosarcoma usually occurs on the shaft of a long bone, but may be seen elsewhere.
(2) Osteoclastoma – a tumour in which the osteoclasts predominate and which looks like a large soap bubble on X-ray. It may be benign or malignant.
(3) Ewing's tumour – a childhood tumour which is thought to arise in the bone marrow and is very sensitive to treatment.

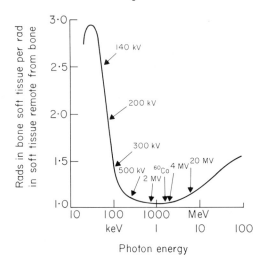

Figure 6. Absorption of radiation in bone at various energies. (By permission of W. J. Meredith and J. B. Massey *The Fundamental Physics of Radiology*, Wright & Sons Ltd, Bristol.

SECONDARY BONE DISEASE

This is by far the most common bone lesion to be treated. Metastatic bone disease is the result of blood-borne metastases and deposits may occur anywhere. The most common sites are:

(1) the spine and pelvis;
(2) the long bones, especially the femur and humerus;
(3) the ribs and skull.

CERTAIN BENIGN BONE AND JOINT CONDITIONS

These may be irradiated as an anti-inflammatory measure, but radiotherapy is not used very much now in this respect because of the risks of late malignant changes.

ACUTE REACTIONS

(1) The acute reactions in bone itself are not particularly noticeable. The noticeable reactions occur in the tissues around the bone.

When there is pain from a metastatic deposit, irradiation may cause an initial increase in the pain due to the increase in the blood

supply to the site after the first one or two treatments. The patient should be warned of this and the analgesia adjusted to cope with it.
(2)   There will be a change in the blood count due to irradiation of the bone marrow. This may be significant if the volume included is large – for example, the spine, the ribs and the long bones.
(3)   There will often be a systemic reaction. This is very noticeable when the spine or the ribs are irradiated.
(4)   There will be a skin reaction and a reaction in other underlying tissues.

LATE RADIATION CHANGES

Bone is a slow-growing tissue and therefore said to be resistant to radiation. However, slow-growing tissue is also slow to repair and if overdosed will not recover. Late changes in bone become apparent 6–12 months after treatment has been given. The changes which take place are dependent on the beam energy and the dose.

The beam energy

As a result of differential absorption, bone irradiated by low-energy radiation may be overdosed.

When bone has been overdosed the cells die and the bone decalcifies. This causes a spontaneous fracture. Fractures of this kind used to be seen in the ribs in the posterior axillary line following irradiation of the chest wall by orthovoltage radiation for carcinoma of the breast. A fracture at this site causes little or no inconvenience; in fact the patient may not even be aware of it. If, however, it were to take place in the mandible or the hip joint, it would be another matter and cause serious disability.

Unless high absorption in bone is required, gamma radiation is used as a means of sparing bone in the irradiated zone.

At 4 MeV (or cobalt 60) the absorption in bone is about equal to the absorption in soft tissue. This has the further advantage of rendering the dose distribution in the body more accurate than at lower energy.

Further large increase in beam energy does not contribute to sparing of bone. The absorption in bone increases again due to pair production and at 20 MeV the differential absorption is much the same as at 250 kV (see Figure 6).

Dosage

The main effects of high dosage in bone are brought about by the radiation effects on the adjacent tissues – the blood vessels, the bone marrow and the periosteum.

The haemopoietic tissue contained within the bone and the periosteum are affected by a lower dose than the bone itself. If the bone is starved of food and oxygen it will die, or will not recover as readily from the radiation effects.

In some cases small pieces of bone become isolated in the healing process and die. This is fairly common in the mouth when irradiation is carried out after the extraction of teeth. A small piece of bone isolated in this manner is called a 'sequestrum', and it will sometimes work out through the tissues. Joints become fibrosed and fixed after high dosage.

Methods of sparing bone

(1)   Avoidance of weight-bearing bone by field arrangement. This is important in planning tumours of pelvic organs, and is the reason for the choice of four oblique fields rather than two laterals.

(2)   The use of short treating distances and/or sealed sources for the treatment of superficial tissue tumours which overlie bone – for example, on the scalp or the back of the hand. The short treating distance reduces the percentage depth dose. A radioactive substance emitting a high-energy beam also reduces the amount of radiation absorbed in the bone.

(3)   Lead shielding of bone not involved in the volume to be irradiated. This also reduces the effect of radiation on the blood.

CARE OF THE PATIENT

The various factors to be considered in the care of the patient with a bone lesion are:

Pain

This is the most important factor, particularly in secondary malignant disease. The pain is constant and demoralising and adequate analgesia must be prescribed until such time as the treatment takes effect and allows it to be reduced or discontinued. When pain is severe the treatment is usually given in large fractions to obtain

maximum relief in the minimum time. Pain due to secondary malignant deposits in bone occurs:
(1) directly over the site, with tenderness on pressure or weight-bearing;
(2) referred pain: spinal deposits cause irritation of the posterior nerve roots and pain is referred to the part served by the nerve.

Pathological fracture

Bone erosion may cause fracture when the bone is subjected to stress. When the bone of the leg is involved, weight-bearing must be avoided and the patient confined to a wheel-chair. If he is allowed to stand, he must use a walking stick or crutch. Walking sticks are available on loan from the hospital. A stick must be adjusted to the correct height for the patient and have a rubber non-slip cap.

Many women do not like to use a stick because it makes them feel 'old', but the need for the support must be impressed on them. A person with a stick is more likely to receive help in the street and is less likely to be pushed and jostled.

If the arm is involved, it should be supported by a sling or plaster back slab. This is a half plaster used as a splint. Before such a support is removed the patient must be positioned so that the part is supported. A long bone may also be 'pinned'. This is an open operation in which a metal plate is inserted alongside the bone and screwed to it.

Neurological damage from cord compression may be caused by the destruction and collapse of a vertebra.

Malaise and nausea

Bone destruction causes nausea and a general feeling of illness due to a rise in the blood calcium. Such symptoms may indicate that the patient is developing bone metastases. If a patient compains consistently of nausea and is generally 'not well' and the symptoms are not thought to be due to a radiation reaction, the medical officer must be informed.

IRRADIATION OF THE
CENTRAL NERVOUS SYSTEM

THE BRAIN

Many intracranial lesions are treated by irradiation. These include:

Primary tumours in the brain

Primary brain tumours arise from the connective tissue in the brain. This is called glial tissue and the tumours are often called gliomata (sing.: glioma). In case of injury to the brain, the glial cells repair the damage and form a scar. This is called gliosis, but the scar tissue is neurologically non-functioning.

(1) Some brain tumours are localised to one part of the brain and are treated by surgery and/or radiotherapy and chemotherapy.

(2) Some brain tumours are multi-focal (arising from more than one place). This necessitates irradiation of the whole brain.

(3) Certain brain tumours disseminate in the cerebrospinal fluid – for example, medulloblastoma and some ependymoma – and therefore the whole of the circulatory area of the cerebrospinal fluid must be treated (the whole brain and spinal canal).

Secondary malignant disease

This can arise from tumours elsewhere, most commonly from the bronchus or the breast. The whole brain is irradiated because the disease is usually multi-focal.

Tumours in other intracranial structures
or organs which are not part of the brain

The pituitary.

Blood vessels (angiomata) and nerve sheath (neurilemoma).

Sarcoma of the skull.

An intracranial lesion usually manifests itself by:

(1) Disruption or alteration of a neurological function. This may indicate the site of the lesion in the brain.

(2) Raised intracranial pressure. The brain has very little room to expand and the growth of a tumour inside the skull will give rise to symptoms of pressure. These include:

(a) headache;

(b) nausea and vomiting;

(c) fits;

(d) papilloedema – a bulging forward of the optic nerves, resulting in loss of definition of the disc margins – this is seen by examination of the eyes with an ophthalmoscope;

(e) decrease in the pulse rate – raised intracranial pressure causes a slow 'bounding' pulse.

THE ACUTE REACTIONS

The acute reactions which follow irradiation of the brain are mainly due to oedema in the surrounding tissues and consequently may cause increase in intracranial pressure. If the patient already has symptoms, the initial treatment reaction may cause a temporary increase of these.

Irradiation of the brain is usually begun with fairly small doses which are increased to full dosage within a few days. The T.P.R. chart must be consulted for changes in the pulse rate, especially at the beginning of the course. As the treatment progresses, the reactions diminish. This is because:

(1) the patient becomes acclimatised;

(2) the lesion begins to reduce in size and intracranial pressure is reduced.

A drug – dexamethasone – is prescribed as required. This is a derivative of cortisone which reduces intracranial pressure by reducing the oedema in the tissues surrounding the tumour.

The skin reaction

This is quite brisk and as the treated area becomes itchy, the patient may scratch. This is difficult to prevent if he is not fully co-operative.

There will be epilation at about 3000 cGy. The head must be kept well powdered and the skin kept under observation for signs of injury. There will be no significant change in the blood count and there is not usually a systemic reaction.

LATE RADIATION CHANGES

Nerve tissue is considered to be resistant to radiation, but the tolerance of any tissue is controlled by its ability to recover from injury.

This limits the tolerance of the brain. When the dose is within tolerance, the tissues recover without apparent damage.

The effects of high dosage become apparent 6–12 months after irradiation. If the tolerance has been exceeded there will be death (necrosis) of the nerve cells. Scarring (gliosis) may take place as the glial cells replace the dead cells and there may therefore be some functional loss. When the volume is small this may be an acceptable side-effect. When the volume is large it may cause the death of the patient.

The dose levels tolerated depend on the volume of tissue irradiated and the part of the brain included. A small volume will tolerate 5000 cGy in 4–5 weeks, with a maximum tissue dose of 5600 cGy, but the mid-brain and hypothalamus are more sensitive to radiation than the frontal and parietal lobes. When the whole brain is treated the dose must be less.

METHODS OF SPARING BRAIN TISSUE

(1)   Planning to limit the amount irradiated by means of a suitable field arrangement and the use of megavoltage radiation for tissue sparing.
(2)   Accuracy of beam direction and good positioning. A radiotherapy department which undertakes the treatment of brain tumours must maintain a high standard of patient positioning and immobilising. Beam directional shells are essential.
(3)   Lead shielding of neurological tissue not included in the lesion volume. This is of particular importance in the treatment of tumours of the neck and post-nasal space when the cord and brain stem may be at risk.

CARE OF THE PATIENT

Primary tumours

Treatment for a primary tumour of the brain is not usually considered palliative, even when the condition of the patient makes a radical plan impractical to begin with. Dramatic response may take place once the treatment is begun.

Secondary tumours

These are usually treated palliatively only, but if the response is good, the policy may be changed to radical. Some of the reasons for treating secondary brain lesions are:

(1) treatment will often prevent the patient from becoming comatose and helpless and therefore a difficult nursing problem;

(2) from the patient's point of view it is good psychology because it makes him feel that something is being done and he is not just left to deteriorate;

(3) it is good for the relatives also, even if they know that the remission obtained is only temporary – the patient may be restored to several months of reasonable life.

The condition of the patient presenting for treatment will depend on the site and extent of the tumour and the neurological and/or physical changes which have been brought about by the tumour.

(1) Many patients are ambulant. They are in fact encouraged to get up and dress as part of the means of returning them to normal living, but they must be treated with care because they are often slow, unsteady on their feet and suffering from visual or other difficulties. Such patients are often depressed and anxious about the outcome of their illness, but will respond to a positive and encouraging attitude on the part of the staff who treat them. Part of their treatment includes physiotherapy and occupational therapy to re-educate and strengthen muscles and improve co-ordination.

(2) A patient with motor disability who is confined to a wheelchair may not always be fully aware of the extent of his disability and think he can do more than he actually can. He is quite likely to stand up if not restrained. A radiographer must never try to handle such patients alone. To do so may risk injury for both the patient and herself. The hemi-plegic patient must have proper support on the treatment room couch to make sure that he does not fall off or injure himself during the time he is alone in the room. These patients benefit a great deal from physiotherapy and occupational therapy. Radiotherapy appointments should be arranged so that they do not miss their sessions in these departments. An important role of the occupational therapist is to teach a disabled patient new ways of doing simple daily tasks, which will help to restore some degree of independence.

(3) Stretcher patients who are unconscious or semi-conscious need the usual care of the conscious or semi-conscious patient. Particular care with regard to respiration is required when a beam directional shell is used. The patient must be closely observed for signs of stridor or change in colour. As treatment progresses and takes effect, an unconscious patient may become very restless and talkative.

Although this is an excellent sign, it can make treating him very difficult. It is very important to remember that a patient who is apparently unconscious and unable to do anything for himself, may still be able to hear and understand all that is said in his presence, so one must always be careful not to say anything that would cause him distress.

(4)   Loss of hair. In many cases the hair will grow again at least partly because of the skin-sparing effect of the high-energy radiation, though it will be about 6 weeks before any signs appear. A wig can be supplied via the Appliance Department to a patient who requires one. This is specially made and the waiting time is about 3 months. Complete epilation is very distressing for a seriously ill patient, especially a woman. When whole brain irradiation is carried out for cerebral metastases, the provision of a wig at short notice is important – the patient cannot wait 3 months; this may be the limit of the remission achieved. In this case, the social services can be asked to help by the provision of money for the purchase of a wig of the patient's own choice. There is a good range of inexpensive ones available from hairdressers and department stores, and as most large hospitals have a visiting hairdresser, there should be no difficulty in having one brought to the ward.

THE SPINAL CORD

Primary lesions of the spinal cord treated by irradiation are comparatively uncommon. They include:

(1)   spinal tumours (cordoma);
(2)   possible spread via the cerebrospinal fluid of tumours of the brain.

The most common situation in which the cord will be irradiated is in the course of treatment of bony metastasis of the vertebrae.

The cord is potentially at risk when a lesion in the neck or upper part of the chest is treated by irradiation – the larynx, post-nasal space, thyroid and even bronchus – because of its proximity to the irradiated area and because, in the neck especially, it is really not far below the surface and the percentage depth dose it receives is high. The part of the cord most likely to be damaged in these cases is the cervical.

Cord compression caused by a tumour, or injury or disease of the vertebrae produces:

Pain

There will be pain in the part affected, especially on movement. Pain will also be felt on gentle pressure with the fingers or by gently thumping with the medial surface of the closed fist. There will also be referred pain along the track of the nerve arising from the affected part:
(1) Cervical: Pain down the arm and in the hand and fingers.
(2) Dorsal: 'Girdle' pain radiating round the chest.
(3) Lumbar: Pain down the legs. Pain in the back of the thigh indicates a lesion of the lower lumbar spine. Pain in the front of the leg may indicate a lesion in the upper lumbar spine and at the side of the thigh, the sacrum.

Sensory changes

Paraesthesia (decreased sensation) and hyperaesthesia (increased sensation) occur in areas served by the nerves arising from the part affected. There may also be changes in temperature discrimination.

Motor impairment

The motor tracts lie at the front of the cord and severe compression will damage them and cause motor impairment below the site of the injury. It will be bilateral.
(1) Cervical – weakness of the hands and arms. With severe damage there will be quadriplegia (loss of use of all four limbs) and/ or death.
(2) Dorsal – paraparesis (weakness, usually of the legs with stumbling on walking), loss of bladder and bowel control. Possible paralysis (complete loss of all function).
(3) Lumbar – the cord ends at the level of L2 and below this a bundle of nerves (cauda equina) passes down to the end of the spinal canal to serve the lower trunk and legs. Cord compression cannot take place but pain and sensory changes may be caused by nerve injury.

THE ACUTE REACTIONS

The acute reactions in the cord itself are not significant. There may be an increase in the neurological symptoms at the beginning of the treatment due to reactions in the tissues surrounding it, but these diminish as treatment progresses.

The skin reaction is of importance, especially if the patient is bed-ridden and it is subject to pressure. Good nursing care is essential.

There will be a systemic reaction and changes in the blood count. These are due to the effects of radiation of the bones of the spine. There may also be a reaction in structures underlying the irradiated part of the spine – for instance, the bowel.

LATE CHANGES

The tolerance of the cord to radiation depends on the length irradiated. The maximum tolerance is 4000 cGy to a length of 15 cm in 4 weeks.

Late radiation change in the cord is called radiation myelitis. This causes 'electric shocks' and tingling in the limbs, when the cord is stretched – for example, on bending the head. The phenomenon is called L'Hermitte's syndrome and it may only be temporary. Severe cord damage causes motor impairment.

These changes are brought about partly by changes in the nerve tissue itself and partly by fibrosis in the tissues around the cord, in particular the blood vessels from which it obtains its blood supply. Fibrosis of the blood vessels is called endarteritis. Damage to nerve tissue by irradiation is irreversible.

METHOD OF REDUCING THE EFFECTS OF RADIATION ON THE CORD

(1)   Localisation of the cord at the time of localisation of the tumour volume. This is essential when lesions of the upper respiratory and alimentary tracts are planned for external irradiation.

(2)   Planning for field arrangements which will avoid the cord or keep the dose received by it low, and by the use of the electron beam for the treatment of lymph nodes of the neck.

(3)   Lead shielding of the cord in close proximity to the lesion, especially when the lesion is to receive a high dose – for example, in the treatment of the larynx, the oesophagus and the post-nasal space.

CARE OF THE PATIENT

When there is any risk of cord compression, every effort is made to prevent disability because severely injured nerves may never recover. When this risk arises from a tumour, a laminectomy and de-compression is carried out with minimum delay. The site of the lesion is determined by a myelogram. This is a diagnostic X-ray procedure in which a small quantity of radio-opaque oil (iodised oil) is introduced into the spinal canal by lumbar puncture and allowed to pass up the canal to the site of the obstruction.

When potential cord damage is due to bony injury or disease, the part of the spine involved must be supported or relieved of weight-bearing. The most common type of support is a cervical collar. This must be made to fit snugly round the neck. If it is too loose it will be no support. In emergency, a folded newspaper and a scarf make a good support.

Patients who are at risk may have to be nursed flat in bed and not permitted to sit up. When treating such patients it is inadvisable to turn them prone. They should be treated by rotating the tube head under the couch. In treating a paralysed or semi-paralysed patient, every care must be assured by the use of cot sides and/or supports on the treatment couch.

IRRADIATION OF THE EYE

The eyes are spared whenever possible because late radiation changes cause impairment and loss of vision. The most sensitive part of the eye is the lens. Doses as low as 150 cGy may induce a cataract.

INDIRECT IRRADIATION OF THE EYE

This may be a risk during the treatment of an unrelated lesion, such as:
(1)   the treatment by superficial radiation of tumours of the eyelids and upper face;
(2)   irradiation of tumours of the brain, post-nasal space and cervical spine, by which the 'exit' dose can contribute some radiation to the contralateral eye;
(3)   irradiation of a lesion of the tongue, cheek or floor of the mouth by sealed sources.

In situations such as these, every attempt is made to reduce the risk by shielding and by suitable field arrangement. When it is impossible to prevent some radiation being received by the eyes, the dose is calculated and/or measured by thermoluminescent dosemeter (T.L.D.) rods. These are extremely small (0.6 cm) and may be taped to the external surface of the eyelid without discomfort.

DIRECT IRRADIATION OF THE EYE

This is unavoidable if the lesion involves the bony socket or a part of the eye itself. It may be necessary to sacrifice the eye in the interest of radical treatment and in this case every effort is made to spare the other eye and reduce the degree of disability.

Lesions of the cornea may be irradiated by strontium 90. This enables a high dose to be delivered to the surface with minimal dosage to the deeper structure. The technique is described below.

THE ACUTE REACTIONS

Conjunctivitis

Quite a small dose of radiation will cause irritation and inflammation of the conjunctiva. There will be increased lachrymation (tears) and the patient will complain of discomfort like 'grit' in the eye. The conjunctiva may also be oedematous.

Keratitis

Inflammation of the cornea – occurs at a higher dose, usually from 2500 to 3000 cGy on megavoltage. The surface of the eye becomes red and inflamed, with visible red veins. The eye is said to be 'injected'. In the later stages the colour darkens to become almost violet. The risk of infection is high and constant vigilance is necessary. Corneal scarring (even without radiotherapy) which may follow corneal ulceration is a common cause of blindness.

Inhibition of the lachrymal gland secretions

At first there is profuse lachrymation, which is the normal response to inflammation in the eye. The tears help to irrigate the eye and reduce the likelihood of infection. As treatment continues the secretions diminish and become sticky and viscous. The eyelids stick together, especially after sleep. The loss of tears increases the risk of infection.

Iritis

Inflammation of the iris with the reduction of the ability to accommodate to light, and photophobia (dislike of light) occurs at about 3000 cGy. The patient may find this very troublesome and dark glasses may be found helpful.

Epilation of the brows and lashes

This occurs as part of the skin reaction at about 2000 cGy. The loss of these removes some of the external protection of the eye. When a child is treated by external megavoltage radiation for retinoblastoma, the exit beam will cause epilation of a patch of hair on the back of the head. The parents must be warned of this. The hair will re-grow.

LATE RADIATION CHANGES

Cataract

Calcification of the lens. This happens up to 1 year after irradiation.
A radiation-induced cataract may be distinguished from a senile cataract because it begins at the back of the lens. A senile cataract begins with several foci of calcification in the lens.

Epiphora

Fibrosis and blockage of the tear duct causing the tears to run down the face. This can be corrected or prevented by consultation with the Eye Department prior to and following treatment. A small probe may be passed down the duct to render it patent.

Shrinkage of the eyeball and glaucoma caused by damage to the anterior chamber

This is very unsightly. Attempts are made to prevent it (see below), but for cosmetic reasons the eye may have to be removed and replaced by a prosthesis.

Fibrosis and shrinkage of the eyelids

This is not likely to happen with megavoltage radiation because of the skin-sparing effect. It is a late effect if high dosage is given at lower energy.

THE CARE OF THE PATIENT

Low energy

When a lesion in the vicinity of the eye is irradiated at low energy, the eye(s) are shielded to give them maximum protection. Internal lead shields are used for superficial radiation. External shielding is used for higher energies (up to 300 kV).

Internal lead eye-shields

Lead eye-shields are made in a range of sizes and are designed to protect the eye from radiation of beam energies up to 3 mm Al H.V.L. (150 KV). The lead thickness is 2 mm. The outside of the shield is painted or varnished to protect the inside of the lids from contact with the lead.

The inside of the shield is lined with a thin layer of plastic to provide a smooth non-toxic surface in contact with the cornea. This layer of plastic also absorbs scattered electrons from the lead and prevents them reaching the eye. Eye-shields may also be made of gold.

Insertion of the shield

Although the eye is not sterile, insertion of the shield is an aseptic procedure.
(1)   An eyeshield of the appropriate size is selected. On the first occasion, more than one size should be prepared. The shield is washed in warm water with soap or detergent. At the same time, it is examined for any damage or roughness on its surface. A small rubber sucker and a round-ended plastic spatula are supplied with the shields. These should also be prepared.
(2)   The shield, sucker and spatula are placed in hibitane for 5 minutes. Eyeshields must never be subjected to heat as this will damage the lining. Neither should they be left too long in hibitane as the cement holding the lining to the lead will be eroded. While the shield is sterilising, an eye tray is prepared.

Eye tray
A sterile tray containing:
Dry gauze.
1% Anaesthetic eyedrops (amethocaine).
Sterile liquid paraffin.
Eye pad and tape.
Plain forceps.

Also required:
100 ml of sterile water or saline.
Medical wipes or soft tissues.

The eye-shield is washed clean of hibitane by pouring the hibitane off and pouring water or saline on. Alternatively, it may be picked up by the forceps, provided it is protected by gauze. Metal forceps are likely to damage the surface. When it is washed, it should be placed on dry gauze.

The sucker and spatula are placed with it. As a safety measure, eye-shields should never be left in fluid because: (a) there may be a doubt as to the nature of the fluid; (b) a sterilising agent will damage the eye if it is mistaken for saline or water; (c) leaving it too long in water may encourage the growth of bacteria.

(3) *Method of use.* Place the patient in the treatment position. Explain the procedure. Anaesthetise the eye:

(a) Tell the patient to look down.
(b) Raise the top lid and put one drop of anaesthetic on the upper part of the eye.
(c) Hold the dropper close to the eye and do not put it on the cornea.
(d) Let the patient close the eye until the stinging wears off and wipe the tears.
(e) Put a second drop in 30 seconds later if needed. The tears will distribute the anaesthetic.

Wash the hands thoroughly: Lubricate the eye shield with one or two drops of paraffin on the inner surface and, holding it by the edges, insert it under the eyelid:

(a) Tell the patient to look down and insert the shield under the upper lid.
(b) Hold it in position and tell the patient to look up.
(c) Pull the lower lid down slightly and allow it to slip over the shield.
(d) Wipe off any oil on the eyelids.

Removal of the shield

There are two methods of removing the shield:

(1) Using the rubber sucker. Press the sucker between the thumb and forefinger to expel the air (and any water that may be inside) and attach it to the surface of the shield. It will stick by suction. Ease the shield out gently, turning it slightly in case there is suction between it and the eye.

(2) Alternatively, raise the upper lid and, telling the patient to look down, slip the edge of the plastic spatula under the edge of the shield. Tell the patient to look up. The shield should slip out.

Inspect the eye after removing the shield and before every treatment.

AFTER-TREATMENT CARE

The eye is anaesthetised and will remain so for up to 2 hours. It is therefore important to protect it from dust or other particles which may damage the eye surface without the patient being aware of it. The eye must be covered with an eye-pad until the anaesthesia wears off. When applying an eye-pad the patient should be asked to close the eyes. It is surprising how many people try to keep the eye open! The patient must also be warned about the reduced field of vision while he is wearing the pad, especially if he has to go out into the street. Furthermore, he should be warned of the dangers of smoking. Cotton eye-pads do not burn, but some are made from synthetic materials and these can ignite. For the same reason, eye-pads must never be secured with Sellotape. Sellotape is very inflammable. This was the subject of a D.H.S.S. Hazard Notice.

After use the eye-shield and its accessories are washed with warm water and soap and replaced in their case.

HIGH-ENERGY (MEGAVOLTAGE)

When it is known the eye will be included in the beam, consultation takes place between the Eye Department and the Radiotherapy Department before treatment begins. The purpose of this is:

(1)   To assess the vision in the eye to be spared. If it is found that the patient will be virtually blind as a result of the treatment the plan may be modified to reduce the disability.

(2)   To gain the co-operation of the Eye Department in dealing with the radiation reactions.

A full explanation must be given to the patient and his co- operation obtained.

During irradiation of the eye, the patient is instructed to keep the eye open. This removes the build-up of the eyelid and reduces the dose to the cornea. At the same time (for cosmetic reasons), an attempt is made to shield the anterior chamber with a thin pencil of lead positioned over the pupil. The patient is instructed to keep the eye fixed on this during the treatment. This, however, may present difficulty unless steps are taken to help him. The eye can only be held in one spot if there is something for it to fix on or a 'frame of reference' of other visible objects. When the beam-defining light of the diaphragm is extinguished or obscured by a wedge or other device, the frame of reference will be gone and the eye will move. To overcome this the lead must be painted with white or fluorescent paint and sufficient additional light provided for it to be easily seen.

CARE OF THE REACTIONS

(1) When the eye becomes sore and there is profuse watering, the patient must be advised against wiping it too often. Rubbing will increase the reaction around the eye and add to the discomfort. The eye should be gently dabbed with a soft tissue to remove the tears. The tissue should be discarded after use. A handkerchief should not be used because of the risk of build-up of bacteria and infection.

(2) As the treatment progresses and the reaction increases, irrigation of the eye may be advised. It is soothing and helps to inhibit infection.

Irrigation of the eyes

Equipment

A plastic or waterproof sheet to protect the pillow.
Towel to collect the excess fluid.
Sterile bowl of warmed saline.
Sterile swabs.
5 ml syringe.
Gloves.

Procedure

The patient is positioned on the couch with the head turned to the affected side. A towel is rolled and placed against the side of the head to collect the fluid. The syringe is filled and the saline allowed to drip into the inner canthus. On no account should any pressure be used to squirt the fluid into the eye. Gentle swabbing of the eyelids to remove congealed mucus may be used.

If necessary, the patient's family may be taught to do this at home, using a saline solution made up from 1 pint of water and 1 teaspoonful of salt, boiled and cooled.

(3) Bacteriostatic eyedrops (Albucid 10%) are prescribed to inhibit

infection when the eye becomes sore.

(4)   Dark glasses will be found restful, but care must be taken to avoid pressure on the skin around the eye.

THE IRRADIATION OF THE EYE BY STRONTIUM 90

Strontium 90 is a beta-emitter with a half-life of 28 years. It disintegrates into yttrium 90, which is also a beta-emitter with a half-life of 64 days. The penetration of the electrons is about 3 mm. Lesions of the cornea are irradiated by strontium, the source being held close to the eye, almost in contact with the corneal surface. The applicator consists of a strontium–silver alloy mounted in a silver 'cup' with a long handle. The cup has a rim which holds the active surface clear of the eye. The active surface is covered with gold foil which filters out the low-energy radiation and protects the surface. When not in use the applicator is stored in a safe for radioactive materials. When removed from the safe it is placed in a shielded container.

Method of use

The eye is anaesthetised and held open by eyelid retractors. The applicator is held in position by hand and the dose rate is obtained from a decay chart. The treatment is timed by a stop watch.

Equipment

1% Anaesthetic eyedrops.

Sterile saline in a dropper bottle, warmed by placing the bottle in a container of hot water.

Eyelid retractors – these are sterilised by autoclaving.

Sterile gauze.

Sterile eye-pad and tape to secure it.

The applicator in a lead container.

A pad of gauze soaked in surgical spirit.

Small hand-mirror.

Stopwatch.

Plain glass protective spectacles for the operator – these are recommended as a protection against stray beta rays.

Procedure

The patient is positioned on the couch with the head as low as is comfortable. Sandbags are placed on either side to steady it and give the radiotherapist a rest for his arms. Care must be taken that overhead lights do not trouble the patient when the eye is held open. A stool is placed at the head of the couch for the operator. The eye is anaesthetised and the eyelid retractors inserted. This is always done by a doctor.

Preparation of the applicator

The applicator is removed from the container and wiped clean by rotating it gently on spirit-soaked gauze. The active surface is then inspected by viewing it in a mirror or through protected glass (lead glass). It must never be viewed unshielded.

CARE OF THE PATIENT

The treatment time is usually short and the patient should be told how long it is to last. During the treatment, sterile saline is instilled into the eye every 30 seconds to prevent corneal drying. After treatment the eye is covered with a sterile pad and the same instructions as for a lead eye-shield apply.

THE TREATMENT OF CHILDREN

The majority of children encountered in the radiotherapy department are under the age of 5 years.

Childhood tumours are embryonic and may be present *in utero*. They are very radiosensitive and the dose levels in treatment are lower than for an adult. A child's tissues are also very radiosensitive. The growth of bone may be arrested by irradiation, causing deformity. This is one of the factors which the radiotherapist must consider as a possible hazard when a child is to be treated. The principal sites of children's tumours are:

(1)   the reticuloendothelial system – leukaemia and lymphoma;
(2)   the genito-urinary system – nephroblastoma (Wilms) and teratoma;
(3)   the central nervous system – medulloblastoma and retinoblastoma, and neuroblastoma.

HYGIENE

Children are susceptible to infection because they have not acquired adult resistance. Childhood illnesses may be brought into the department. Hygiene in the treatment room is of the utmost importance, not only for the safety of the child, but for other patients who may be put at risk.

CO-OPERATION DURING TREATMENT

Small children certainly present problems of co-operation, and this is sometimes heightened by an anxious parent communicating fears to the child. The treatment procedure must be fully explained to the parents, in order to gain their assistance. Time spent of cajolery and bribery is not wasted on the patient. Children can be remarkably good and co-operative once they know that they are not going to be hurt. No attempt must be made to restrain a child forcibly. Potential injury includes slipped epiphysis and greenstick fracture.

If the child is too young to understand or does not co-operate, it is safer and less time-consuming to sedate him. Sedation is arranged in consultation with the paediatrician. Sedatives must be prescribed by a doctor. The drug may be given in syrup which the child takes readily. It may also be given by injection. This is quicker and more certain than oral sedation but sometimes has the disadvantage of upsetting the child and making him frightened of the treatment.

Oral sedation is administered at a predetermined time before treatment (usually about 1 hour) and the child is brought to the department before it becomes fully effective and put to rest in a screened-off cubicle. Sedation given by injection is administered in the department. The time taken for it to be effective is short, and the degree of sedation is light. The child is placed on a stretcher as soon as he is unconscious, from where he is transferred to the treatment couch. After treatment he is again placed on the stretcher in the recovery position and returned to the cubicle where he remains with nursing supervision until fully conscious.

CARE IN THE TREATMENT ROOM

Close observation is essential while the child is being treated, but it is inadvisable for personnel to remain in the room, even with a shield, while the treatment is being given. Care must be taken that he cannot fall from the couch while he is alone in the room. A sedated child may suddenly regain consciousness and become restless. Webbing straps round the child's body and the couch top are secure and cannot cause injury. If setting-up is done with a front pointer, great care must be taken, when the pointer is close to the skin that the child does not make an involuntary movement. It is safer to set the correct distance to one side of the child and remove the pointer before positioning him under the treatment unit.

REACTIONS TO TREATMENT

A child's tolerance of radiation is lower than that of an adult. The dosage, both total and in fractions, is much less. Apart from the greater sensitivity of the tissues, it must be realised that the volume of tissue irradiated, especially in thoracic and abdominal tumours, is much greater in proportion to the size of the body than in an adult. Furthermore, the percentage depth dose received by other organs (the gut for instance), will be much greater in the smaller body of the child.

THE SYSTEMIC REACTION

This makes the child irritable and miserable. There is loss of appetite and tiredness. It is a mistake to try to make the child eat when he does not want to. If possible, food should be available on demand, with plenty of 'treats' to tempt the appetite. The parents' co-operation is invaluable in this respect. There should be plenty of fluids, especially those with food value. Anti-emetics and vitamins are given as required.

There will be changes in the blood count. In childhood, the differential proportions are about equal. Adult proportions are reached at puberty.

TREATMENT BY SMALL SEALED SOURCES

Techniques which employ small radioactive sources close to the tumour are called brachytherapy (from the Greek, *brachy*, short) because the treating distance is from 1 to 2 cm. Another term which may be encountered is plesiotherapy (Greek, *plesio*, near). These techniques have certain advantages over external radiation techniques.

(1)   A large dose of high-energy radiation can be given to a small volume of tissue close to the source. At the same time, because of the short treating distance, the percentage depth dose received by tissue outside the treatment volume is low.

(2)   The use of sources which emit high-energy radiation is sparing of bone and cartilage.

(3)   The course of treatment is completed in a fairly short time. For example, gynaecological treatment may be completed in 24–48 hours. This is important when bed occupancy has to be considered.

(4)   The techniques are capable of great accuracy.

The disadvantages of using radioactive sources are:
(1)   Radiation hazard to personnel.
(2)   The risk of possible loss of the sources.

These risks are minimised by:
(1)   Strict rules relating to storage, custody, record-keeping and transport. The care and custody of radioactive sources is the responsibility of the radium custodian who is in turn responsible to the chief physicist and the radiotherapist. Regulations related to storage and handling are set out in the Code of Practice for the Protection of Persons against Ionising Radiations arising from Medical and Dental Use (H.M.S.O.). These rules are supplemented by such local rules as may be thought necessary in wards and departments where the sources are used.

(2)   Correct handling techniques. It is essential that personnel handling radioactive sources have training, and practice with dummy sources to learn the techniques and reduce the handling time factor. The correct tools and shielded work benches must always be used. Remote after-loading and manual after-loading techniques in the treatment of patients reduce the hazard to personnel to a minimum. These are techniques in which applicators to carry the sources are positioned in or on the patient and the sources introduced afterwards. Sophisticated fully automatic after-loading systems are available, mainly for gynaecological work. Manual after-loading systems are simpler, the sources being introduced by hand.

(3)   The protection of personnel by the use of shielding, of distance and of time. Patients are confined to shielded rooms or cubicles while the sources are *in situ*, and supervision is by pro-

tected viewing window or by closed-circuit television. A radiation warning sign must be displayed at the entrance. In some cases the sources can be withdrawn to enable nursing procedures to be carried out. When this cannot be done, full use must be made of body shields, distance from the sources and time factor. Radiation monitors must be worn. Rotation of staff also reduces the hazard to individuals.

RADIOACTIVE MATERIALS IN USE

For many years, radium 226 was the element employed. Radium is a source of gamma radiation with a half-life of over 1000 years, but its major disadvantage is the production of radon gas as one of its decay products. For this reason it has been withdrawn from medical use. This has been made possible by the production of other radioactive materials in the nuclear reactor, the most commonly used of which are caesium 137, cobalt 60 and iridium 192. Radium techniques have been adapted to these materials with good results. Their disadvantage are their shorter half-lives of 28 years, 5.3 years and 74 days respectively.

METHODS OF USE

Moulds

A mould is a device made to carry the sources for the treatment of tumours of superficial tissues on the surface of the body and in the mouth. Among the factors governing the choice of this technique are:
(1)   poor tolerance of underlying tissue – for example, cartilage in the pinna of the ear;
(2)   the risk of over-radiation of underlying bone if low-energy radiation and a longer treating distance were to be used.

A mould is made of Perspex or dental acrylic. These materials are rigid and of low density. The procedure for making the mould is basically the same as that used for a beam directional shell, the material being moulded on to a plaster model of the area. The mould is made in two parts: a base which is fitted accurately on the patient and a separate section to carry the sources which is secured once the base is in place.

The arrangement of the sources on the mould is calculated from published dosage rules and the method by which the sources are secured must offer 100 per cent security against loss while it is in use. Regular inspections must be carried out each time the mould is put on or removed, to ensure that they are intact.

Care of the patient

A mould is worn for a calculated number of hours (usually 5–6) on a calculated number of days (6–8). During the time it is worn, the patient is confined to a shielded room or cubicle. The treatment, though not arduous, may be boring and provision must be made for the patient's entertainment and comfort. He should be advised in advance to bring in any books, magazines or writing materials he may wish. Some of these can be provided. A woman can bring knitting or sewing. A radio, preferably with headphones, and television can also be made available.

The patient must have means of summoning a member of the staff in case of need. He is not permitted to leave the room unsupervised, partly because of the radiation hazard, but also in case of loss of the sources. He must be advised to go to the lavatory before the treatment begins.

Meals and refreshments are provided. It is usual to remove the mould in order to let him eat his meal in freedom. The part of the mould in contact with the skin must be cleaned thoroughly after each session and wiped with antiseptic solution. Moulds used in the mouth are moistened with mouthwash before being inserted, and thoroughly cleaned after use.

The treated area must be cleaned and dressed as required. Skin care is the same as that for external irradiation. Where there is a mucosal reaction in the mouth, attention must be paid to mouth hygiene and diet.

Dosage records

The only record required for a mould is the date and time on each occasion it is fitted or removed. This must be recorded with meticulous accuracy until the total calculated time is complete. A shielded trolley must be kept in the room to receive the sources when they are removed.

Interstitial treatment

Radioactive sources may be implanted into the tissues. The principal sites for this method of treatment are in the mouth – the tongue and the buccal surface of the cheek – and the anal canal.

The treatment is very uncomfortable, both during the course and immediately following the removal of the implant, but the end-result is good. It is curative and there is good functional recovery. Patient care and good nursing are essential.

Pre-treatment care

(1)   A full explanation of what is to be done to gain the patient's co-operation.
(2)   Attention to the patient's general condition. This includes correction of anaemia and treatment of any infection by antibiotics. Dental care may be required.

During the treatment, respiratory infections may complicate the nursing, and therefore chest conditions are investigated. Smoking should be discontinued.

Procedure

The implant volume is assessed and the distribution calculated from published dosage data. A plan is made for reference during the procedure. Iridium wire is generally used for implants in the mouth. Needles may be used at other sites. These are prepared by threading with silk threads. Sterilising is carried out by autoclaving, chemical means or by ultrasound. An implant is always carried out in theatre under general anaesthetic. After the implant, the positions of the sources are verified by radiography. An implant carries quite a high risk of exposure for the surgeon/radiotherapist and the theatre staff, and safety procedures must be strictly followed in theatre. A manual after-loading system is available for iridium, in which a plastic tube is implanted and the iridium introduced manually when the position has been verified.

Care of the patient

The mouth

(1) Pain and discomfort. Analgesia is given as required. Local analgesics such as aspirin mucilage are given prior to meals to relieve discomfort on eating.

(2) T.P.R. There is a possibility of infection at the site of the implant if proper care is not taken. There is also the possibility of bronchopneumonia if the patient has other respiratory conditions, and medical suction must be on hand.

(3) Mouth hygiene is important, both as an anti-infection measure and for comfort. Mouth-washes are given before meals and the mouth is cleaned after meals. At the same time, the implant is inspected and any movement of the sources reported.

Mouth tray:
Sinus forceps to remove debris.
Plain forceps.
Gauze swabs and dental rolls.
Wooden tongue depressors.
Soft toothbrush.
Tepid mouth-wash.
Torch.
Disposal bag.

Procedure:
   The mouth is swabbed gently, using swabs held by forceps while the tongue depressor is used to hold the tissues apart. After cleaning the patient is given a drink of water.

(4) Diet: the diet must not be entirely fluid because this will not provide sufficient nourishment. The patient must not be allowed to feel hungry. The diet should be soft, high-protein, with plenty of fluids and extra vitamins. A spoon should be provided for eating, and a straw for drinking.

(5) Communication: a pencil and paper must be available if the patient finds talking difficult. He must also have means of summoning the staff.

The anal canal

In some centres a temporary colostomy is performed to isolate the anal canal during treatment. This is quite a big operation. In other centres, bowel movement is eliminated by preparation before treatment.

The patient is admitted 3 days before the implant. An aperient is given on the day of admission and the patient put on a low-residue diet. The day before the implant he has a bowel wash-out and 10 ml of mist. kaolin et morph. This ensures no bowel action for at least 7 days. During the period of the treatment he is kept on a low-residue diet.

Care of the patient while the implant is in position is similar to that described for the mouth:
(1)   control of pain and discomfort;
(2)   monitoring of possible infection;
(3)   cleaning of the site and inspection of the implant.

Radiation safety

Radiation safety precautions already listed must be followed. In addition to these, visiting of the patient is restricted. No dressings or linen may be removed from the room unless they have been monitored or all the radioactive sources are accounted for.

Removal of the implanted sources

Implanted sources are removed in theatre. This is because:
(1)   anaesthesia is required because of pain – the implant is removed easily because of local necrosis in the immediate vicinity;
(2)   there may be haemorrhage.

Late radiation changes

There will be local fibrosis and loss of secretions in the mucosa at the site of the implant. In the mouth there may be local changes in the bone of the jaw if it has been highly dosed. There may also be some effect on the teeth.

The effect on the salivary glands will be minimal because of sparing by low percentage depth dose. In the anal canal, local fibrosis may cause constipation which must be controlled by diet and aperients.

Intracavitary applicators

The principal use for intracavitary applicators is the treatment of

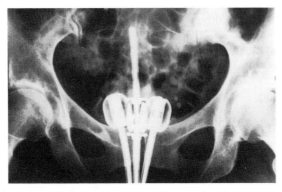

Figure 7. Intracavitary irradiation of the cervix uteri. (Radiograph reproduced by permission of the Radiotherapy Department, Royal Free Hospital, London, and of Amersham International, PLC.).

tumours of the cervix uteri (see Figure 7). In the early stages of the disease, intracavitary irradiation alone is used. In the later stages, when there is possible involvement of the pelvic lymph nodes, intracavitary irradiation is supplemented by external irradiation. The success rate is good. The primary diagnosis may be made by cervical smear and confirmed by E.U.A. and biopsy. At the same time the extent of the disease is assessed and the method of treatment decided.

Treatment systems

There are several systems for intracavitary irradiation, all of them basically the same, being based on well-established radium systems.
(1) The Amersham after-loading system is widely used. One of its advantages is that it is a direct conversion from the Manchester radium system. It is therefore easy to apply both technically and from the point of view of well-established published dosage data. It is flexible and relatively inexpensive. The sources are caesium 137 and after-loading is manual.
(2) The Cathedron uses cobalt 60 sources and has fully automatic after-loading. The higher dose rate obtained by using cobalt 60 reduces the treating times. In some centres patients are treated as outpatients with fractionated dosage. Mild sedation is given prior to the treatment.
   The disadvantage of the Cathetron is that it is a major installation and its use is limited to one type of treatment. It is therefore expen-

sive. Other automatic after-loading systems using caesium 137 are also available.

Pre-treatment care

Anaemia

Heavy or intermittent blood loss is associated with tumours of the cervix and many patients are anaemic. This must be corrected.

Infection

The cervix uteri is the site of many infections. These must be treated. Bladder infection, when present, must also be treated.

Psychological preparation

A full explanation of what is to be done helps to prepare the patient and gain her co-operation. In the majority of cases, insertion is carried out under general anaesthetic. The patient is admitted 24 hours before the procedure and theatre preparation includes an aperient and bowel wash-out.

Insertion procedure (Amersham system)

The applicators to contain the sources are made of high-grade plastic and are supplied in sterilised packs. They are disposable after use. They are available in three sizes and comprise:
(1)   two catheters 25 cm in length to be positioned in the cervix and two ovoids to hold them in place;
(2)   a third catheter 32 cm long to be positioned in the uterine canal where it is held by washers and spacers between the ovoids.

After the insertion, Vaseline gauze packing is inserted to hold the assembly in place and free of the anterior wall of the rectum, which has a low tolerance of radiation.

At the same time, a low-energy radioactive source is introduced into the central catheter (uterine canal) and the dose received by the bladder and by the anterior wall of the rectum measured by an ionisation chamber probe. From this the total dose received by these organs over the whole period of the treatment may be calculated. To reduce the risk of disturbance of the assembly during treatment the patient is catheterised.

Verification of the position of the assembly is obtained by radiography. Antero-posterior and lateral radiographs are taken, using magnification markers to enable the dose distribution to be calculated.

When insertion and verification are complete, the sources are introduced manually. This is done in the ward and by a member of the radiotherapy staff. The time of the introduction must be accurately recorded.

The sources are contained in long stainless-steel springs and held in place by retaining screws in the ends of the catheters. The average treatment time is 24 hours.

Care of the patient during treatment

(1)   Discomfort. There may be discomfort from the pack. Analgesia is prescribed as required.

(2)   Systemic reaction. The patient may have nausea. Anti-emetics are given as required.

(3)   Diet. The patient may not feel like eating. A low-residue light diet with plenty of fluids is required.

(4)   Infection. There is a possibility of infection at the treatment site. This may give rise to pyrexia (raised temperature). It is not usually of significance because pyrexia will not be apparent until about 24 hours after the insertion, by which time it will be due for removal. Antibiotics may be prescribed if it is thought necessary.

(5)   The patient is confined to bed and the position of the insertion inspected at intervals. Any change in the position must be reported immediately. There must be a shielded trolley and forceps in the room in case of premature removal.

(6)   Personnel safety. Certain after-loading systems enable the sources to be withdrawn during nursing procedures. Failing this, the safety procedures set out above must be followed.

After-treatment care

The sources are removed at the calculated time by a member of the radiotherapy staff. The pack and the applicators are removed in the ward. A sterile vaginal pack must be available in case of bleeding. After removal, the patient is allowed to get up and have a warm bath.

During the following few days there may be cystitis and diarrhoea due to the radiation reaction. Specific remedies are prescribed and fluid intake should be increased. There will also be vaginal discharge due to the reaction at the treated site. Douching is advised. This also reduces infection.

Loss of radioactive sources

The loss of a radioactive source is a potential major hazard. As soon as any loss is discovered it must be reported to the Physics Department and to the radiotherapist. The physicists will immediately institute a search, using a radiation detector. The procedure to be followed will depend on the circumstances of the loss but the following rules are general:

(1) close the area to all unauthorised personnel;
(2) do not let anything be removed from the area;
(3) do not let the patient leave the hospital – the source may have been swallowed or concealed deliberately;
(4) if it is suspected that the source has been removed in linen or dressings, inform the laundry manager and the incinerator staff;
(5) if it is suspected that it has been lost in the lavatory or wastepipe of the wash basin, inform the hospital engineer.

Index

175

Index